Conversations with Young People in Family Mediation

Conversations with Young People in Family Mediation

Lisa Parkinson
Family Mediator and Trainer

Bloomsbury Professional

LONDON • DUBLIN • EDINBURGH • NEW YORK • NEW DELHI • SYDNEY

BLOOMSBURY PROFESSIONAL

Bloomsbury Publishing Plc
50 Bedford Square, London, WC1B 3DP, UK
1385 Broadway, New York, NY 10018, USA
29 Earlsfort Terrace, Dublin 2, Ireland

British Library Cataloguing-in-Publication Data

A catalogue record for this book is available from the British Library.

ISBN: PB: 978 1 52652 958 9
Epdf 978 1 52652 960 2
Epub 978 1 52652 959 6

Typeset by Evolution Design and Digital (Kent)
Printed and bound by CPI Group (UK) Ltd, Croydon, CR0 4YY

To find out more about our authors and books visit www.bloomsburyprofessional.com. Here you will find extracts, author information, details of forthcoming events and the option to sign up for our newsletters

Foreword

How would adults feel if decisions were made about *them* without their voices even being heard? And how would adults feel about being heard by proxy – having a relative or a professional assuming that they can speak for them? I think that the answers to that are plain. They would feel that they had been treated unfairly, whatever the eventual outcome might be. Procedural fairness matters and being heard is an essential of it. That applies to children, just as much as it applies to adults – probably even more so when the decisions are about what is best for the young people concerned. From a very early age, young people develop an innate and strong sense of what is fair. In schools and in homes they are used to insisting that they be heard. They are encouraged to learn about the world and express opinions about it. Why should they not be heard when major decisions are being made about them, decisions that will affect them for the rest of their lives?

The purpose of this book is to help mediators and family lawyers gain a fuller understanding of the importance and significant benefits of including young people in mediation. It is written by one of the most respected and recognised family mediators in this country. The work and commitment of Lisa Parkinson has lain at the heart of the development of our mediation system. We all owe Lisa a huge debt of gratitude for her steadfast work in showing that there is a better and more inclusive way than litigation and that Family litigation, with all its destructive potential, should be a last resort.

I commend this book to you, strongly. It is very well written and structured. It traces the slow historical development in our understanding that children should be seen *and* heard. It summarises the research and the legal context by which that development has evolved and explains where matters are now. It gives invaluable advice about how young people should be included within the mediation process. Lisa imparts her unequalled wisdom and experience in this field about the resilience of children and gives heart-felt accounts from young people about their experiences and wishes to be heard.

Of particular interest to me are the passages where Lisa gives practical advice to mediators about how they should go about the inclusion of young people within the process. Adults tend to think that they know how to listen to children. To do so, actively, however, is a skill on which we all need to work. As Lisa says in Chapter 6, listening to children is not about plying them with questions and extracting answers from them in order to confirm our own pre-existing views or on a 'need to know' basis. Similarly, we all like to think that we understand how to demonstrate diversity and inclusivity in our work, whereas that understanding is never static and has to be the subject of constant awareness and study; Chapter 4 in this book, on diversity and inclusivity, is of considerable importance, therefore.

Thank you, Lisa, for writing this book and for all that you have done for mediation in this country.

HHJ Stephen Wildblood KC
9 November 2023.

Preface

The first challenge I faced in writing this book was its terminology. In the 1980s and 90s, a process called 'child consultation' was undertaken by a minority of mediators, generally with a background in social work and family therapy, who believed that children should be offered the opportunity to have a say in mediation. The United Nations Convention on the Rights of the Child 1989 encouraged a gradual shift towards 'child-inclusive mediation', as it came to be known. However, adolescents object to being called 'children'. 'We are people too and shouldn't be treated like low-lifes just because we are younger. I think kids deserve the same kind of respect that we are expected to give to so-called adults'.[1] 'Child-inclusive mediation' is also a misleading term, since many children are not included.[2] The acronym, CIM, easily confused with CIN (Children in Need), is virtually meaningless when pronounced as SIM. I prefer 'Conversations with young people in mediation', but it lacks a neat acronym. 'Children in Mediation' (ChiM) is therefore used from Chapter 3 onwards to describe an important change of approach. Previously, the emphasis was on ascertaining the wishes and feelings of the child, mainly as a source of information for adults. Now, the aim is to offer children and young people a voice in their own right, because their views matter and they have the right to be heard.

Following the Report of the Family Solutions Group, *What About Me?* Reframing *Support for Families following Parental Separation*, the Family Solutions Children's Group undertook two consultations to explore children's experience and needs during and following their parents' separation or divorce.[3] The first consultation sought the views of professionals from different disciplines with extensive experience of working with children. In the second consultation, members of the UK Youth Parliament were asked about their experience and needs when their parents separated. Based on these consultations, the Report of the Family Solutions Children's Group, *What About Me? A Child's Right to Matter,* was launched on 13 November 2023 with a reception at the House of Commons. Edward Timpson MP wrote in his foreword to the Report that his experience as a family law practitioner, as former Minister for Children and Families and as chair of CAFCASS, while also coming from a family who fostered children, all showed that children and young people need to be able to access help at critical points in their lives and have their voices heard, when they wish.

Almost without exception, children and young people want their views and suggestions to be heard and taken into account when arrangements are made for them during major transitions in their family life. Their positive accounts of talking with a qualified family mediator are supported by research findings referred to in the final chapter of this book. Researchers report that children's participation in mediation helped them to feel valued and respected, while also facilitating parental agreement on arrangements that are likely to work better in practice than

1 O'Quigley A *Listening to Children's Views* Joseph Rowntree Foundation 2000 p. 30
2 See Chapter 4
3 Family Solutions Group What About Me? Reframing Support for Families following Parental Separation November 2020; What About Me? A Child's Right to Matter November 2023

a child arrangements order made by the court. Family mediators have a vital role in helping children and separated parents to listen to each other and work things out together. It is very encouraging to note the growing interest among family mediators in many countries in acquiring further training and sharing experience in this special area of mediation work.

Lisa Parkinson
Bristol
January 2024

Acknowledgements

I am extremely fortunate that Philippa Johnson agreed to be editor of this book. Philippa is a very experienced editor of family law reports, as well as being an accredited and highly skilled family mediator and a member and former chair of the Family Mediators Association Board of Trustees. Philippa has a keen eye for clarity and structure and her helpful recommendations encouraged many improvements when I was trying to see the whole wood while also focusing on different trees.

I owe special thanks to Philippa for introducing me to Andy Hill, her former colleague at Sweet & Maxwell and now Head of Practitioner Publishing at Bloomsbury. Andy Hill and Jane Bradford are the most supportive and helpful publishers one could wish for. I was very aware of the sensitivity needed when writing about mediators' awareness and understanding of gradual shifts and changes in a young person's sense of gender identity and sexual orientation. Andy Hill asked Eris Young, author of *They, Them, Their – a guide to nonbinary and genderqueer identities* (Jessica Kingsley 2019), to read and comment on Chapter 8. I am extremely grateful to Eris for her very helpful advice on key points and on language matters.

Young people's observations and comments bring the book to life. I thank my mediator colleagues most warmly for their accounts of conversations with children and quotes from the children (anonymised, with names changed). Foremost among them is Cathy Frances, founder and director of the award-winning Stratford Family Mediation. Cathy has a special gift for connecting with young people, who often tell her that she is the one person who listens to them. Cathy also has the empathy and skills to help parents take their children's messages on board, so that parents become more attuned to their children's needs and perspectives and family arrangements then work more smoothly.

There is growing interest in other countries in children's participation in mediation. In pre-Covid times, I enjoyed annual visits to Italy for many years to take part in workshops and conferences organised by Ana María Sanchez Duran and her colleagues at Mediamente in Florence, and also in the mediation diploma course directed by Professor Costanza Marzotto at the Catholic University in Milan. The Covid epidemic opened up opportunities to provide ChiM training and consultancy online. At the invitation of my fellow grandmothers in mediation, Annie Babu in France and Linda Bérubé in Quebec, I gave an online module on ChiM (in French) in their mediation training programme in 2023 in Guadeloupe, arranged by the University of the West Antilles. I just longed to be with them in person. But training online creates opportunities to work with experienced co-trainers who organise role-plays in their own language and assess mediators' competencies, using the Family Mediation Council's requirements for ChiM training and practice. In the past year, I have provided ChiM training in Ukraine, Latvia and Lithuania and I am very grateful to Tetyana Bilyk in Ukraine, to Faila Abbasova in Latvia and to Odeta Inte in Lithuania for the pleasure and privilege of working with them. I should also like to thank Fidana Alieva, pioneer of mediation in Kyrgyzstan, for introducing me to International Mediation Campus in Germany, an online training organisation with connections in around seventy countries worldwide. At a World Mediation

Forum conference in Buenos Aires some years ago, I met María Paola Felibert. Paola and her co-mediator use the same model of ChiM and we value our continuing exchanges of experience and reflections.

ChiM mediators everywhere are greatly encouraged by the findings of the research carried out by Professor Anne Barlow, Dr Jan Ewing and their colleagues at the University of Exeter School of Law. The benefits reported by children and young people who talked with a ChiM-qualified family mediator are quoted in the final chapter of this book. We learn and understand so much more when we listen to children and young people, and also in discussion with other mediators and researchers. The residential weekends on Mediation, Science and the Arts which Neil Robinson and I organise every two years at Ilam Hall in Derbyshire provide inspiration and rich nourishment in contributions from the UK and other countries, including Ireland, Sweden, Switzerland and the former Soviet State of Georgia. The importance of hearing the voice of the child has been highlighted by the Family Solutions Group (FSG). Helen Adam, chair of the FSG, and Carlie Norris, co-author, are high acclaimed for their recent report, *What About Me? A Child's Right to Matter*.

At home, my husband, Tim, has given me his constant support over a great many years and his computing skills have saved me on many occasions. I am happy that he enjoys the company of our mediator friends as much as I do. Our daughter, Diana, principal researcher and evaluator at the Centre of Expertise on child sexual abuse, based in London under the wing of Barnardo's, provided links to reports and advice on statistics, particularly in the chapter on diversity and inclusivity.

I owe so much to my family, friends and colleagues. However, the omissions, errors and other failings in this book are entirely my own responsibility.

Lisa Parkinson
Bristol
January 2024

Biographical note

With an Honours degree in Modern Languages from Oxford University, Lisa studied social sciences and qualified in social work at the universities of London and Bristol. In the 1970s, the adversarial legal system intensified and prolonged conflict between divorcing parents with harmful impact on their children. Children struggling with emotional and behavioural difficulties were liable to be placed in a special school for 'maladjusted children'. It was the system that was maladjusted, rather than the children. Following the recommendations of the Finer Report in 1974 for conciliation in family courts instead of litigation, Lisa joined a small group of professionals in Bristol to set up the first out-of-court family mediation service. The service opened in May 1979 with a grant from the Nuffield Foundation. In the 1980s, Lisa took part in another pilot scheme in London with five family lawyers, including Henry Brown and John Cornwell (who founded the family lawyers' association, Resolution). This led to the founding of the Family Mediators Association (FMA) in December 1988. Lisa was appointed FMA's director and with Henry Brown as legal consultant, training courses in mediation on all issues in separation and divorce, including finance and property, were run in London and regionally from 1989 onwards. Lisa was also a member of the Committee on the Future of the Legal Profession (Marre Report, 1988), a founder member of World Mediation Forum (inaugural conference, Madrid 1996) and the Hague Group of Experts on the Guide to Good Practice in Cross-Border Mediation (July 2012). Lisa took part in international conferences and gave training in Europe and also in Moscow, Morocco, North and South America, Guadeloupe, Kazakhstan, South Africa, Turkey and Réunion Island in the Indian Ocean. To increase opportunities for children and young people to explain their views and concerns in mediation, Lisa convened a working group of child-inclusive mediation trainers in 2016, whose recommendations for additional training and standards of competency were implemented by the Family Mediation Council the following year. These changes led to a significant increase in children's participation in mediation. Lisa was awarded the Significant Achievement Award in the National Mediation Awards 2022.

Contents

Chapter 1

Hearing the voice of the child

Introduction

This chapter traces the gradual shift from the late 20th century onwards from regarding children as objects of parental care and possession, who should be 'seen and not heard', to recognising the child as a subject of legal rights, including the right to have a voice and be heard on matters concerning the child's life and well-being. The United Nations Convention on the Rights of the Child 1989 was a major turning-point. In the same year, the new Children Act 1989 in England and Wales placed a statutory obligation on the courts, when dealing with private law children matters, to take account of the wishes and feelings of the child.[1] In Europe, the European Convention on the Exercise of Children's Rights came into force on 1 July 2000, while the Regulation known as 'Brussels II' (Regulation on Jurisdiction in Matrimonial Matters and Matters of Parental Responsibility) came into force on 1 March 2001. Brussels II introduced uniform jurisdictional rules throughout the European Union (EU), apart from Denmark, with almost automatic recognition of matrimonial judgements granted by the courts of Member States. The Council of Europe Recommendation 2003 states that the child 'should also be heard in the mediation process because he or she is recognised as having rights. Children should be allowed their say if a solution is to be found that is genuinely in their best interests.'[2] Brussels II Revised (in March 2005) upholds the right of the child to be heard, in accordance with his or her age and maturity, on matters relating to parental responsibility over the child. It also provides uniform recognition of decisions by family courts in Member States on parental responsibility for children of married or unmarried parents, including stepchildren. In 2010, the Council of Europe's Guidelines on Child-Friendly Justice (2010) state that the child's rights should be guaranteed both in in-court and out-of-court proceedings, such as mediation.[3] In England and Wales, the Report of the Family Solutions Group, *What About Me? Reframing Support for Families following Parental Separation,* made a renewed call for the voice of the child to be heard and for information on support services to be made available to children and young people.[4] However, the question remains as to whether, and if so, to what extent, these directives and recommendations have actually changed practice on hearing the voice of the child, both in and out of court.

1 Children Act 1989, s 1(3) and 4.
2 Council of Europe, Recommendation *Family mediation and gender equality* 2003 No. 1639, 2003, para 6.
3 Council of Europe *Guidelines on Child-Friendly Justice* 2010, IV, para 26.
4 Family Solutions Group Report *What About Me? Reframing Support for Families following Parental Separation,* 12 November 2020.

Children should be seen and not heard

In the 15th century, children, particularly girls and young women, were expected to remain silent until spoken to. *Mirk's festial – a Collection of Homilies* by a clergyman, Rev. John Mirk, advised that 'a *mayde should be seen but not herd*'.[5] In the 17th century, John Locke urged parents to '*be sure then to establish the authority of the father as soon as he (the child) is capable of submission and can understand in whose power he is.*'[6] Children were taught to regard their parents as '*their lords, their absolute governors*' and be in awe of them.[7] Locke considered that '*children's minds [are] as easily turned this or that way as water itself.*'[8] Children In working class families were put to work at an early age. In his tour of Great Britain in the 18th century, Daniel Defoe came across young children spinning cloth in their parents' cottages in the Yorkshire dales. '*Hardly anything above four years old but its hands were sufficient for its support.*'[9] Children laboured for long hours in factories and coal mines until Lord Althorp's Factories Act of 1833 set limits to their working hours. In contrast, children in upper-class families led sheltered lives, brought up by their governess and looked after by nursemaids. Boys were sent to public schools such as Eton or Harrow, while girls were educated at home by their governess. Beatrix Potter, author of 'The Tale of Peter Rabbit' and other well loved stories for children, was born in 1866 into a wealthy upper-class family. She spent her childhood in the nursery with her governess, visiting her parents downstairs at set times. The view that '*children should be seen and not heard*' was still widely held in the 19th and much of the 20th century.

Women's Rights

Before children could be recognised as individuals with minds and needs of their own, a battle had to be fought to establish the rights of women. Although Darwin valued the female assistants who helped him in his groundbreaking work on the origin of species, he believed that women were inferior to men and that a woman's role was to look after her children and manage domestic matters. '*Man is more courageous, pugnacious and energetic than woman and has a more inventive genius. His brain is absolutely larger. Women are inferior intellectually.*' Throughout the 19th century, women were not accepted as 'persons' in the eyes of the law. It was not until 1929 that the Judicial Committee of the Privy Council held that the term 'persons' could include women.[10]

The Married Women's Property Act 1870 permitted a married woman to inherit property and be the legal owner of money that she earned, but she was not permitted to leave her husband's home. If she left, her husband could enter the home of any relative or friend with whom she sought refuge, carry her off by force and sue her for 'restitution of conjugal rights'. A husband could divorce his wife, but a wife could not defend herself or be represented by a lawyer and she

5 Mirk, J, *Mirk's Festial – a Collection of Homilies* c 1430, republished in *English Sermons 1100 – 1500* (Early English Text Society, Kegan Paul 1905).
6 John Locke, *Some Thoughts Concerning Education* 1693, 40.
7 Ibid.
8 Ibid.
9 Defoe, DA, *Tour Through the Whole Island of Great Britain 1724-27.*
10 Lady Hale *Spider Woman – A Life* (Penguin Books 2021) 179.

could not divorce her husband, however badly he mistreated her. The custody of children of the marriage belonged automatically to the father. A mother could have custody only of an illegitimate child, or if she were 'awarded' custody by a court order. A mother who had committed adultery had no prospect of being granted custody of her children. In 1837, after leaving her drunken and abusive husband, an MP and failed barrister, Caroline Norton fought unsuccessfully for access to her three young sons. Her widely publicised campaign led to the Custody of Infants Act 1839, which allowed a mother to apply for a court order for custody of her children under seven years old and for access to her older children.[11] The Divorce and Matrimonial Causes Act 1857 gave women the right to apply for a decree of divorce or nullity. After the First World War, social attitudes began to change. The Sex Disqualification (Removal) Act 1919 opened the professions and universities to women. Oxford University awarded the first degrees to women in 1920, whereas female graduates at Cambridge had to wait until 1948 to gain a BA (Cantab), instead of the embarrassing 'BA (tit)', meaning 'titular'. In 1928, women over 21 gained the right to vote in a general election.

Custody of children in private law proceedings

Under the Guardianship of Infants Act 1925, the courts were directed in proceedings involving the custody or upbringing of a child to have regard to 'the welfare of the child as its first and paramount consideration'. Mothers sought parity with fathers and achieved recognition of their equal status under the Guardianship of Minors Act 1973, which recognised the equal rights and authority of both parents and permitted these rights to be exercised jointly or separately. Shared parenting after separation was not encouraged, however. Some commentators argued that when parents separated, the children should remain in the care of one parent who should take all decisions concerning their upbringing and welfare, including whether the other parent should have access to the child.[12] Divorce petitioners applied for sole custody, believing this to be the normal arrangement, and the courts rubber-stamped their application, thus maintaining sole custody as the norm. In September 1980, only 2% of custody orders were for joint custody. It was generally considered that if parents were in conflict, joint custody was unworkable, while if they were co-operative, joint custody was unnecessary. The Law Commission's Review of Child Custody Law revealed widely divergent views among judges on the value of a joint custody order and great variations in their use.[13] In 1985, 42% of custody orders in Truro were for joint custody, compared with 8% in Colchester and 4% in Romford. In a case that went to the Court of Appeal, an eight-year-old girl had been spending alternate weeks with each parent. The Court of Appeal declared that this arrangement was 'prima facie wrong', although it had worked for five years with no apparent detriment to the child, whose own views and wishes received minimal, if any, attention.[14] Divorcing parents who became embroiled in disputes over their children fought for sole custody as a prize to be won or lost. The winner claimed victory, while the losing parent was demoted to the status of secondary parent, or even non-parent. The term, 'one-parent family', used by the

11 Norton, C, *English Laws for Women in the 19th century* (Dodo Press); Fraser, A *The Case of the Married Woman: Caroline Norton and her Fight for Women's Justice* (Pegasus Books, 2022)
12 Goldstein, Freud and Solnit, *Beyond the Best Interests of the Child* (The Free Press, 1973).
13 Law Commission, Review of Child Law: Custody, Working Paper 96, HMSO 1986.
14 Times Law Reports, *R v R*, 28 May 1986.

Finer Committee,[15] suggested that the other parent was disposable, 'like paper plates or plastic cutlery'.[16]

The Children Act 1989

Under the leadership of Brenda Hoggett, who, as Baroness Hale of Richmond, later became President of the Supreme Court, the Law Commission's Review of Child Custody Law[17] led to a major reform of child law in England and Wales in the form of the Children Act 1989. The new statute called for the child's wishes and feelings to be taken into account in decisions concerning the child. The term 'custody' was replaced by 'parental responsibility', signifying that parents have responsibilities and duties towards their child, rather than ownership of their child, and that in all matters concerning the child, the child's welfare and best interests should be the court's paramount concern. However, 30 years after the Children Act came into force, the media continue to refer to a parent having 'custody' of a child[18] and many parents talk about intending to apply for 'custody'. They are surprised to learn that 'custody' no longer exists in family law and that both parents continue to hold parental responsibility after divorce (unless the court orders otherwise).

United Nations Convention on the Rights of the Child 1989

The UN Convention on the Rights of the Child, signed by the UK in 1991, overturned the presumption that parents have absolute authority over their child. Article 12 (1) of the Convention states that

> 'States Parties shall assure to the child who is capable of forming his or her own views the right to express those views freely in all matters affecting the child, the views of the child should be given due weight in accordance with the child's age and maturity.[19] For this purpose, the child shall be provided the opportunity in any judicial or administrative proceedings affecting the child to be heard, either directly, or through a representative or an appropriate body, in a manner consistent with the procedural rules of national law'.[20] Under Article 13, 'the child shall have the right to freedom of expression; to seek, receive and impart information and ideas of all kinds, regardless of frontiers, either orally, in writing or in print, in the form of art, or through any media of the child's choice.'[21]

The importance of the child's views being heard and taken into account in all decisions and arrangements affecting the child is recognised, not only in Articles 12 and 13, but throughout the whole Convention. Recognition of the child's right to be heard gives the child a sense of autonomy, independence, heightened social

15 Report of the Committee on One-Parent Families, 'Finer Report', HMSO 1974.
16 Parkinson, L *Joint Custody* October 1981, One Parent Times, 10.
17 See n 13 above.
18 See, eg, *The Guardian*, 23 March 2023.
19 UN Convention on the Rights of the Child, Art 12(1).
20 Ibid Art 12(2).
21 Ibid Art 13(1).

competence and resilience.[22] In a report for UNICEF, Gerison Lansdown points out that 'it is important to understand clearly what Article 12 does and does not say. It does not give children the right to autonomy ... [or to] ride roughshod over the rights of their parents. However, it does introduce a radical and profound challenge to traditional attitudes, which assume that children should be seen and not heard.'[23] Listening to children and valuing their views and ideas leads to decisions that work better in practice than those taken by adults without consulting the child concerned.[24] 'Children have a body of experience and knowledge that is unique to their situation.'[25] In a House of Lords judgment in 2006, Baroness Hale said:

> 'There is a growing understanding of the importance of listening to the children involved in children's cases. It is the child, more than anyone else, who will have to live with what the court decides. Those who do listen to children understand that they often have a view that is quite distinct from that of the person looking after them. They are quite capable of being moral actors in their own right. Just as the adults may have to do what the court decides, whether they like it or not, so may the child. But that is no more reason for failing to hear what the child has to say than it is for refusing to hear the parents' views'.[26]

Article 9(3) of the Convention states that a child who is separated from one or both parents has the right to maintain personal relationships and direct contact with both parents on a regular basis, except where this is shown to be contrary to the child's best interests. In a case that went to the Court of Appeal, a child aged five had been brought up believing that her mother's cohabitee was her father. The court took the view that the child had the right to know the identity of her birth father, who was seeking contact with his daughter. There was no question over his paternity and the mother accepted that the child should be told who her true father was and have contact with him.[27]

To what extent is the voice of the child heard?

International recognition of the child's right to be heard does not ensure that the child's voice is heard in practice. Noting that children's views are not systematically taken into account in decisions concerning the child, the UN Committee on the Rights of the Child is calling for stronger action 'to promote the meaningful and empowered participation of children, including children in disadvantaged situations, within the family, community, schools, and include children in decision-making in all matters relating to children.'[28]

Few children and young people have the confidence to ask to speak to a judge who is making decisions that concern them. The court is an intimidating environment

22 Richman, JM and Bowen, LG, 'School failure: an interactional ecological developmental perspective' in Fraser, M (ed), *Risk and Resilience in Childhood: an ecological perspective* (NASW Press, Washington DC 1997) 95-116.
23 Lansdown, G, *Promoting children's participation in democratic decision-making* (UNICEF/ Innocenti, Florence, Italy 2001) www.unicef-irc.org/publications/pdf/insight6.pdf, s 1.2.
24 See Ch 12.
25 Ibid s 1 (4f).
26 *Re D (A Child) (Abduction: Rights of Custody)* [2006] UKHL 51, [2007] 1 AC 619.
27 *Re R (a Minor) (Contact) (1993)*
28 UN Committee on the Rights of the Child, *Report and Concluding Observations* 2 June 2023.

and although the judge may meet with the child in chambers, young children express fears that if they speak to the judge, the judge could find them guilty in some way and even send them to prison. After hearing the child, the judge may be obliged to explain to parents that the court's decision has been influenced by hearing the child's views and wishes, bringing the risk of repercussions on the child from parents who feel let down. Some judges also question whether they have the necessary training and expertise to talk with a child or young person in such circumstances.

Rather than hearing the child themselves, family court judges in England and Wales are likely to ask the Children and Family Court Advisory and Support Service (Cafcass) to ascertain the child's wishes and feelings, to consider the child's best interests and make recommendations to the court. Cafcass advisers are overloaded with safeguarding enquiries and one study found that 60% of children who were the subject of an enquiry were seen for half an hour or less.[29] A study of public and private law child proceedings commissioned by the Ministry of Justice to inform family justice developments[30] found that 10% of divorces involved child-related proceedings and were likely to be high conflict cases. The sample consisted of 602 children involved in 393 private law cases. The father was the applicant in 77% of these applications and the mother in 20%. The study reported that 53% of cases involved 1–4 court hearings, 31% involved 5–9 hearings and 16% involved 10 or more hearings. Cases resulting in a final order lasted on average 51 weeks, almost a year in the child's life. If there are no interim arrangements, it may be very difficult to rebuild a child-parent relationship after such a long break. In cases where litigation continues for up to six or even eight years, the loss of the child-parent relationship may be irreparable. A recent report found that court proceedings in child-related cases take on average 45 weeks.[31] The President of the Family Division expressed concern at the Family Law Conference in Jersey in 2021 that 'in a substantial number of cases coming before the family courts, the court process is not one that either adds value to the welfare of the child or is in any way beneficial for the parents. In some cases it may simply provide a pitch and a referee for them to play out further rounds in their adult contest'.[32]

The Children Act 2004, 'Every Child Matters', underlines the responsibility of all those working with children to help safeguard them and protect their welfare. The Act introduced a Private Law Programme encouraging in-court conciliation on child-related matters with the aim of promoting early settlement and avoiding protracted litigation. In-court conciliation, in which a Cafcass adviser acting as conciliator met with parents or guardians to encourage agreement, was found to be very successful in enabling the majority of disputes to be settled by consent at the First Dispute Resolution Hearing. The time Cafcass spent on in-court conciliation increased and the number of reports reduced.[33] In-court conciliation was also found to be effective in avoiding continuing litigation. However, a study reported

29 Hunt J, *Parental Perspectives on the Family Justice System in England and Wales: a review of research* December 2009, Report for the Family Justice Council.

30 Cassidy, D and Davey, S, *Family Justice Children's Proceedings, Research Summary* (Ministry of Justice 2011) 5/11.

31 Supporting earlier resolution of private family law arrangements – Ministry of Justice Consultation April 2023, www.gov.uk.

32 McFarlane, A, *Supporting Families in Conflict – There is a better way*, Address to the Jersey Family Law Conference 2021, www.judiciary.uk/announcements/speech-by-the-president-of-the-family-division-supporting-families-in-conflict-there-is-a-better-way.

33 Cafcass Annual Report 2006–2007.

that 'it was rare for children to take part in conciliation directly. Hence the child's views would typically be presented through one or both parents'.[34] Sixty-one per cent of the parents or carers who were consulted considered that the session had focused on their children's needs, but among those who reached agreement, fewer than half (48%) thought the agreement was in their child's best interests. Cafcass advisers continue to do impressive 'conciliation' work, both at the first hearing and in their Improving Child and Family Arrangements service, but they only do so when invited by the court. The focus of their work is primarily on providing reports and the term 'conciliation' did not appear in a recent report.

Family court advisers and child experts appointed by the court have a crucial role in ascertaining children's views and advising the court on their best interests, but by the time they become involved, parents' positions may have become polarised and children's conflicting loyalties may prevent them from talking freely. Family members, children as well as adults, need help at an early stage of separation and divorce to communicate safely and listen to each other, so that they can work out their own solutions without turning to the court. Help and support provided at an early stage can lead to better outcomes and avoid high costs later on.

The Family Justice Review

The Family Justice Review was set up in 2010 by the Ministry of Justice 'to examine the effectiveness of the family justice system and the outcomes it delivers, and to make recommendations for reform'.[35] Recognising that 'long and complicated legal processes are emotionally and financially draining for parents and distressing for children', the Review called for a system 'which allows families to reach easy, simple and efficient agreements which are in the best interests of the children, whilst protecting children and vulnerable adults from risks of harm. Family mediation and similar support should be used as far as possible to support individuals themselves to reach agreements about arrangements, rather than having an arrangement imposed by the courts'.[36]

The Office of the Children's Commissioner was commissioned to seek the views of children and young people with recent experience of public or private child law proceedings, so that their views could be reflected in the final report of the Family Justice Review. The young people said that from the earliest stage they wanted more information about the process of decision-making, the roles of those involved and the ways in which they could make their own views known. They said that the lack of information available to them was a major barrier to their involvement and meaningful engagement. They wanted to know whether and if so, how, Article 12 of the UN Convention on the Rights of the Child would apply in practice and make a difference in the context of family court proceedings. A 16-year-old boy said: 'All I wanted was someone to talk to – I never had anyone.' A 13-year-old said: 'I don't

34 Trinder, L et al., *Making Contact happen or making contact work? The process and outcomes of in-court conciliation* (DCA Research Series 3/06, 2006) 89.
35 Family Justice Review, Terms of Reference 2010.
36 ibid.

think our parents knew how we were feeling. I feel glad that I've been able to talk I've finally got to express what I feel. I think adults should talk to kids more.'[37]

The Final Report of the Family Justice Review (Norgrove Report) stated:

> 'It is now generally accepted … that it must be right for children and young people to be given every opportunity to have their voices heard in cases that are about them. Yet many children and young people may not even be aware that a case is underway, let alone have their views heard as part of it … Children's interests are central to the operation of the family justice system. Decisions should take the wishes of children into account and children should know what is happening and why.'

The Review called for:

> 'more child focus and better training for professionals to make sure children's views are heard … Children and young people should be given age appropriate information to explain what is happening when they are involved in cases. They should as early as possible be supported to make their views known and older children should be offered a menu of options to lay out the ways in which they could – if they wish – do this'.[38]

The Review also reported that 'many people … pointed out that informing and consulting children is a much more difficult exercise in private law than it is in public law, where the tandem model provides representation for the child in all cases'.[39]

The opportunity for a child to talk with a mediator is one of the options that should be offered, with full explanation of its principles, aims and benefits. Information should be provided to parents and to children and young people themselves. ChildLine reported that children's calls to their helpline provide:

> 'a very persuasive argument in favour of a mediation service which includes children … (it) could be of considerable help to children, as well as to parents, in managing the feelings that threaten to overwhelm them … Children are perfectly able to enter into discussions about the future, so long as they are not being asked to choose in an atmosphere of acute conflict where they feel caught in the middle'.[40]

In mediation, separating parents are encouraged to focus on their children's needs and well-being, rather than on settling old scores and fighting 'win-or-lose battles'. When parents co-operate in their children's best interests and children have the opportunity to express their views and wishes, follow-up studies show that arrangements worked out by family members themselves work better and last longer than those made by a court order.[41]

---

37 *Do More than Listen. Act*, Consultation Response from the Office of the Children's Commissioner, July 2011, 22 and 13.
38 Family Justice Review, Executive Summary, para 9.
39 Ibid para 4.134.
40 Childline Report, *Unhappy Parents, Unhappy Children* 1998, 23.
41 See Ch 12.

The impact of LASPO

However, two months after endorsing the recommendations of the Family Justice Review, the government passed the Legal Aid, Sentencing and Punishment of Offenders Act 2012 (LASPO). Following LASPO's withdrawal of legal aid for nearly all family matters, solicitors no longer needed to refer clients seeking legal aid to an information and assessment meeting ('MIAM') with a qualified mediator to consider mediation and other ways of resolving matters. It was not made clear to the public, nor even to family lawyers, that legal aid was still available for MIAMs. In 2010, the Bristol branch of the Family Mediators Association received nearly 800 referrals and was recording a steady increase in private and publicly funded mediations. One year after LASPO came into force, the Bristol mediation service closed, along with many other mediation services. The number of MIAMs dropped from 30,655 in 2012/13 to 13,390 in 2013/14.[42]

Mediation Task Force

The government killed mediation and then tried to resurrect it. In an effort to repair the damage caused by LASPO, a Mediation Task Force was set up in the spring of 2014 under the chairmanship of David Norgrove, who had chaired the Family Justice Review. The final report of the Task Force, published in June 2014,[43] recommended that ways of seeking children's views on decisions about their future should be urgently reviewed and that a small interdisciplinary group should be established to draw up standards for mediators' training and guidelines for practice. The Task Force also recommended that the Charter drawn up by the Family Justice Young People's Board should be updated to include mediation and provide a coherent blueprint for hearing children's voices. The Children and Families Act 2014 established the long-awaited unified Family Court and introduced the Child Arrangements Programme (CAP) and Family Procedure Rules, with renewed emphasis on dispute resolution: 'The CAP is designed to assist families to reach safe agreements where possible out of the court setting ... [since] it is well recognised that negotiated agreements between adults enhance long-term co-operation and are better for the children concerned'. The Child Arrangements Programme called for the voice of the child to be heard.[44]

The Rt Hon Simon Hughes, then Minister of State for Justice and Civil Liberties, was a strong champion of the child's right to be heard. In his speech to the Family Justice Young People's Board 'Voice of the Child' Conference on 24 July 2014,[45] Simon Hughes announced his intended policy that all children aged ten and over who were the subject of family proceedings should have the opportunity to speak to the judge, either in person or in an appropriate way, or to talk with another qualified professional. 'Children and young people of ten and over will therefore be given the chance to make known their views in person or if preferred in another way.' Simon Hughes called for a 'non-legal presumption'

42 FMC-Response-to-NAO-Consultation-on-Legal-Aid-July-2023.pdf familymediationcouncil.org.uk.
43 Mediation Task Force Report Ministry of Justice, June 2014.
44 Child Arrangements Programme, s 4, 12B.
45 Rt Hon. Simon Hughes MP, Speech at the Family Justice Young People's Board 'Voice of the Child' Conference, 22 July 2014.

that children and young people aged ten and above should be able to have their voices heard, if they so wish. Although the government gave its support to this presumption, a subsequent freedom of information enquiry found that action on the presumption had been shelved. Undeterred, Simon Hughes set up the Voice of the Child Dispute Resolution Advisory Group 'to ensure that the necessary steps are taken to promote child-inclusive practice and that the voices of children and young people are heard in all private family law proceedings that impact on them'.[46] The Voice of the Child group arranged a workshop with the Family Justice Young People's Board (FJYPB), a group of around 40 children and young people aged eight and over with experience of the family justice system, to seek their views on the child's voice being heard in out of court resolution processes. Members of the young people's group expressed strong views about the importance of children being provided with child-friendly information and having opportunities to express their views. Bethany, a 19-year-old member of the group, said: 'It is vital to hear the child's voice about a case in which a decision is made that may ultimately affect them for the rest of their lives. In my case, I had to wait four years before my voice was heard and I was considered to be too young to know my own mind and I was lumped together with my younger sister.'[47] Members of the FJYPB thought it should be the norm for children to talk with a mediator, not just an option. One young person commented: 'Mediation would be more successful if children and young people are included.'

Family Solutions Group Report, '*What About Me?*'

The Family Solutions Group (FSG) was set up as a subgroup of the Private Law Working Group to give 'fresh and focused attention to improving the experiences of, and providing opportunities for, separating families away from the Family Court'.[48] The FSG Report, *What About Me? Reframing Support for Families following Parental Separation,* proposed that family law professionals, mediators and helping agencies should form local Hubs to help separating parents and family members navigate critical transitions in their lives. Directly accessible, community-based services should be made available to children and young people, during and following parental separation, providing them with information, consultation, support and representation. The FSG noted the continuing failure to hear the voice of the child and made a renewed call for a legal presumption that all children aged ten and above should be offered the opportunity to have their voices heard directly in all processes for resolving issues between parents, including mediation. A webinar in which the FSG presented their recommendations was introduced by the President of the Family Division and attended by nearly 500 family law professionals, indicating a high level of concern about the harmful consequences for children when parental conflict is prolonged. The FSG website includes a link to a short film, *What About Me*?, with quotes from children and young people.[49]

46 Voice of the Child Advisory Group Report, March 2015.
47 Voice of the Child: children to be more clearly heard in decisions about their future – 2015 www.gov.uk.
48 Family Solutions Group Report, *What About Me? Reframing Support for Families following Parental Separation* 12 November 2020
49 www.judiciary.uk/publications/what-about-me-reframing-support-for-families-following-parental-separation/.

Building on the FSG's recommendations, Cafcass and Cafcass Cymru launched pilot projects in Dorset and North Wales in March 2022 in partnership with the Ministry of Justice, to provide a more effective triage system signposting separated parents to mediation, relationship advice, Parenting Plans and other services, rather than setting a date for a court hearing. When a court decision is needed, these projects seek to make the proceedings less adversarial, reduce delays and improve the experience of separated parents/carers and their children by enabling children to be heard at an earlier stage. Cafcass is developing these Pathway Projects with judges, mediation specialists, domestic abuse support providers and family lawyers and the projects are being evaluated over a two-year period. Cafcass also runs 12-week Positive Co-parenting programmes for parents and carers and provides a free phone-line, Hear to Listen, for children and young people. In February 2023, the Cafcass Family Forum – a group of parents, carers and family members with experience of family court proceedings – issued Top Tips for parents and professionals involved in family proceedings. These tips include 'Court proceedings should be the last resort. Think of other ways to resolve the issues such as mediation before going to court. If your child is struggling emotionally, speak to professionals and seek support from their school or GP.'[50]

Normalising child participation

The 13th European Forum on the Rights of the Child 2020 ended with these words from the children who participated: 'We need a strategy that is inclusive of all children and that supports children in vulnerable situations and we need a strategy that supports and promotes our right to participate in decisions that affect us. Because nothing should be decided for children without children. It's time to normalise child participation.'

50 www.cafcass.gov.uk/2023/02/09/cafcass-publishes-new-tips-from-its-family-forum-for-parents-and-professionals-involved-in-the-family-court/.

Chapter 2

Hearing the voice of the child in family mediation

Hearing the voice of the child in mediations in the UK

In the 1980s and 90s, family mediators were mainly concerned with issues between separating and divorcing couples. Children's views and wishes were rarely sought.[1] Parents were anxious to shield their children from distress and mediators were doubtful about, or even opposed to, children's direct involvement. Many mediators were trained in the structured, settlement-seeking approach developed by Fisher and Ury at Harvard Business School.[2] This model was not designed for mediating on matters concerning children. Consequently, mediation was solution-focused, rather than child-focused, with little attention given to 'the child's involvement, or lack of involvement, in the processes in which parents formalise their separation and reorganise their own and their children's lives'.[3] Many mediators were concerned that talking with children on their own and informing parents of their child's views and wishes would 'disempower' parents, instead of 'empowering' them. It was claimed by some mediators (without supporting evidence) that 'the disadvantages of involving children directly or indirectly in the mediation process far outweigh any advantages'.[4] Other mediators, often with a background in family therapy, took a different view that 'children's opinions should be taken into account, since their lives are drastically affected by custody and access decisions and by the level and duration of parental conflict. If they are directly involved in conciliation, they may have useful comments to offer … and may have a great deal of insight into their families' difficulties'.[5] A project run by Mediation in Divorce in Surrey, *Listening to Young People,* was designed to give children the voice they otherwise lacked.

> 'Previously, it was always possible to involve children directly in mediation, but in practice it rarely used to happen. We were cautious about undermining the authority of parents in mediation and we tended to think that the best people

1 Hayes, S, 'Family Mediators in the UK – A Survey of Practice' [2002] *Fam Law* 760; Murch, M and Keehan, G, 'The Voice of the Child in Private Family Law Proceedings' [2003] *Family Law*.
2 Fisher, R and Ury, W, *Getting to Yes – Negotiating Agreement Without Giving In* (Houghton-Mifflin, New York, 1981); Haynes, J, *Divorce Mediation* (Springer Publishing, 1981)
3 Timms, J, 'The Silent Majority – the Position of Children Involved in the Divorce and Separation of their Parents' April 2003 Child Care in Practice.
4 Roberts, M, *Mediation in Family Disputes* (Community Care Practice Handbooks, 1988)102.
5 Parkinson, L, *Conciliation in Separation and Divorce* (Croom Helm, 1986) 165, 179, reissued by Routledge 2023; 'Child-Inclusive Family Mediation' [2006] *Family Law* 483–488; Pendlebury, M, 'Divorce and Separation: listening to children and young people in mediation' [2008] *Family Law* 1255.

> to talk to children were usually their parents. Several factors caused us to review our policy, including … research findings resulting from interviews with children whose parents had separated or divorced. Offering children a more direct voice in the mediation process is not so much a change of policy, more a change of emphasis. We present the idea to parents in a more positive way, and at an earlier stage. We don't consider children's participation as an exceptional option, but rather as something we actively encourage, because we see that most children appreciate the opportunity to be heard directly.'[6]

In 2014, the Mapping Paths to Family Justice study reported that in most mediations, children's interests tended to recede into the background, with the voice of the child notably unheard.[7] Few parents in the research sample had considered whether their children should be involved directly. The small number who considered it had usually turned it down, because of their concerns that it would cause their child emotional distress. In the sample of 56 parents who had taken part in mediation, only two parents had consented to their child's involvement. The researchers identified four main barriers: (1) the financial cost to parents of additional mediation sessions; (2) lack of information and understanding of children's rights and needs among separated parents and their professional advisors; (3) parents' concerns to protect their children from distress and shield them from what the parents considered to be adult issues; and (4) mediators' lack of confidence in talking with children. The researchers recommended that there should be more opportunities for children's voices to be heard in mediation.

Mediation in international cross-border cases

International conventions and legislation call for the child's voice to be heard in public and private family law proceedings and also in international cases of parental child abduction across national borders. Mediators in cross-border cases look for training and guidelines on the application of international conventions and directives. In April 2006, the Permanent Bureau of the Hague Conference on Private International Law was asked by its Members to 'prepare a feasibility study on cross-border mediation in family matters, including the possible development of an instrument on the subject'. The Permanent Bureau convened an international group of experts who met in The Hague to advise on a Guide to Good Practice on Mediation in the context of the 1980 Child Abduction Convention.[8] Guidelines for parents and family law professionals on mediation in cross-border child abduction cases were also produced by International Social Service (ISS), based in Geneva.[9] MiKK in Germany has trained many mediators in cross-border mediation and organised a training programme for mediators in Ukraine provided by international trainers, including Tetyana Bilyk in Ukraine on trauma-informed practice.[10]

6 Mediation in Divorce, 2004.

7 Barlow, A et al, *Mapping Paths to Family Justice – Briefing Paper and Report on Key Findings* (Universities of Exeter and Kent, June 2014).

8 Hague Conference, *Guide to Good Practice on Mediation in the context of the 1980 Child Abduction Convention,* July 2012 in English and French editions.

9 www.iss-ssi.org.

10 Mediation bei internationalen Kindschaftskonflikten: Paul, C and Kiesewetter, S, *Cross-border Family Mediation* (Wolfgang Metzner Verlag, 2011); Paul, C, Kiesewetter, S and Khalaf-Newsome, I (eds), 3rd edn. 2023.

Enforcement of agreements is a key concern in Hague Convention cases. When mediation in cross-border cases concerning children leads to agreement between the parents or carers of the child, it is vital to have jurisdictional rules in place that ensure that the mediated agreement will be recognised, not only in the state hearing the application but also recognised and upheld in the state where the agreement needs to take effect. In African and Middle Eastern countries that are not signatories to the Hague Conventions, cross-border cases may be heard by religious and secular courts with their own laws and principles. The Council of Europe's 7th Conference on Family Law and International Family Mediation was held in Strasbourg in March 2009 in response to the need for harmonisation and co-operation in the growing field of international family mediation. The conference was hailed as an opportunity to review the activities of international organisations in this field, to create synergies and avoid duplication. Dr Jelena Arsic, a lawyer and family mediator from Serbia, spoke about family mediation with bi-national couples in former Yugoslavia. Professor Albert Fiadjoe from the University of the West Indies spoke about family mediation in the Caribbean, where the Family Court of Trinidad and Tobago had introduced procedural reforms drawn from New Zealand to encourage referral to mediation and counselling services.[11]

Hearing the voice of the child in cross-border cases

Under the 1980 Hague Child Abduction Convention, 'the court may refuse to order the return of the child if it finds that the child objects to being returned and has attained an age and degree of maturity at which it is appropriate to take account of its views.'[12] Listening to the child's views and wishes is extremely important in considering whether 'there is a grave risk that his or her return would expose the child to physical or psychological harm or would otherwise place the child in an intolerable situation.'[13] When Hague Conference court proceedings are commenced, the court with jurisdiction may refer the parents to one of the non-governmental, national and bi-national agencies that provide international cross-border mediation in parental abduction cases. These agencies include *reunite* in the UK, International Social Service based in Switzerland and MiKK in Germany. Reunite's report on their pilot project in international cross-border mediation, published in October 2006, explained that a child consultant talks with the child and conveys the child's wishes and views to co-mediators, who share them with parents in mediation and encourage their consideration. Reunite reported that children taken to another country were likely to lose their contact and relationship with the left-behind parent and with other family members as well. Many children experienced profound dislocation. When the court concluded that it was in the child's best interests to remain in the country to which they had been removed, the child's relationship with the non-resident parent was unlikely to be maintained, owing to travel costs and other difficulties.

11 Fiadjoe, A, *Family mediation in the Caribbean,* Paper given at the Council of Europe's 7th European Conference on Family Law on International Family Mediation, Strasbourg, March 2009.

12 Hague Conference 1980 Child Abduction Convention, Art 2.

13 ibid Art 13(1)b.

Developing a co-ordinated approach to children's participation in mediation

Until relatively recently, family mediators' practice in meeting and talking with children was limited and unregulated. The term 'Direct Child Consultation' (DCC), used by National Family Mediation, implied that the main purpose was to seek the child's views and wishes, rather than as an opportunity 'to unblock channels of communication between children and parents so that parents and children can listen to each other and hear each other with more understanding'.[14] As a first step towards clarifying policy and developing a more coordinated approach to mediators' practice, the UK College of Family Mediators (which preceded the Family Mediation Council) invited a working group of three mediators (only one of whom had experience of meeting with children in mediation) to draw up recommendations on DCC policy and practice. The group's recommendations formed the basis of the UK College's Policy and Practice Guidelines on Children, Young People and Family Mediation, published in 2002, which stated that 'the UK College has a positive policy that family mediators should actively encourage parents and/or other participants in mediation:

- to talk with and listen to their children so that the decisions parents make about arrangements for their children are reached in the light of an understanding of each child's perspective, and
- to consider the different ways in which children may be involved or consulted, including, when appropriate, offering opportunities for them to take part directly in discussions with the mediator/s'.[15]

The Guidelines set out the pre-requisites and factors that should be taken into account in assessing the suitability of consulting with a child, including the child's age, family culture and circumstances, and the level of conflict between the parents. The Guidelines also identified specific competencies for direct child consultation, listing additional areas of knowledge and skills. The Guidelines were circulated to mediators, but they attracted little interest and were soon forgotten.

The UK College was replaced in 2007 by the Family Mediation Council (FMC). Four of the five member organisations of the FMC – the College of Mediators, the Family Mediators Association, National Family Mediation and Resolution – provided training in child consultation, but it was not known whether their training covered similar ground or whether it differed in content, methods and objectives. In 2015, the Voice of the Child Group undertook a survey of FMC mediators trained in direct consultation with children.[16] The findings suggested that mediators who talked with children were using a range of different approaches, without any systematic approach or regulation of practice. The Voice of the Child Group recommended that pilot schemes should be set up to evaluate different approaches. Guidelines were produced on principles and requirements for children's participation and for mediators' training and practice, with the aim of 'embedding a changing culture where the voice of the children within mediation will become the norm (for

14 Parkinson, L, *Family Mediation* (Sweet & Maxwell, 1997) 202.
15 UK College of Family Mediators, Children, Young People and Family Mediation – Policy and Practice Guidelines 2000, revised and extended 2002
16 See Ch 1 (n 45).

children aged ten and over)'.[17] However, the pilot projects were not set up and the new norm did not materialise.

In March 2016, frustrated by the continuing lack of progress, trainers from five member associations of the Family Mediation Council (FMC), all of whom had experience in providing training in child-inclusive mediation, agreed to meet together to develop a unified approach. Family Law in Practice (FLIP) provided the venue for a series of meetings which took place over a 15-month period. There was a high degree of consensus at these meetings and further progress was made through the circulation of draft documents. The FMC heard that these meetings were taking place and invited the trainers' group to become a formal FMC working group (with travel expenses paid!) and to submit recommendations for mediators' training, practice and professional practice consultancy. At the end of May 2017, the trainers' group submitted four papers to the FMC relating to children's participation in mediation:

Paper 1 Definition, Objectives, Principles and Requirements.

Paper 2 Competencies for mediators and methods of assessment.

Paper 3 Requirements for Course Providers.

Paper 4 Transitional and ongoing professional development requirements for mediators and professional practice consultants (PPCs).

The trainers' group defined child-inclusive mediation as follows:

> 'Child-inclusive mediation provides opportunities for children and young people to have their voices heard directly during the process of mediation, to help them feel respected and listened to and, at their request, to assist parents or carers to receive, understand and take account of the child's messages and/or suggestions regarding decisions and arrangements for the child.'

There was consensus that the core principles of mediation set out in the FMC Code of Practice and in the Guide to Family Mediation in England and Wales[18] should apply equally to children's participation.

Applying the core principles of mediation to hearing the voice of the child

1 Voluntary participation

The participation of the child or young person requires the informed consent of both parents, or those holding parental responsibility. With their consent, the child or young person is invited to talk about their views and concerns, but not pressed to accept. The courts do not have power to order the child's participation.

17 Voice of the Child Group Final Report, 2015, Introduction, see also Ch 4, Age of the Child.
18 Family Mediation Council/Family Justice Council, *Guide to Family Mediation in England and Wales* April 2014, issued with the support of the President of the Family Division

After mediation has been considered at initial information and assessment meetings and found to be safe and suitable, parents and carers who accept mediation are asked to sign the Agreement to Mediate. In explaining the process of mediation, the mediator should explain the child's right to be consulted and encourage parents or guardians to consider different ways in which their child may be heard, if the child is mature enough to express views and make suggestions, and wishes to do so. If the preferred option is for the child to be invited to talk with a qualified mediator, the parents or guardians are asked to sign a letter of consent in which they confirm their willingness to consider their child's views and wishes and undertake not to coach the child on what to say, nor question or reproach the child afterwards.

Since children of sufficient maturity have the right to be heard, if they wish, the need for parental consent may be questioned. Why should parents or carers be able to deprive a child of their legal rights? The Voice of the Child Group considered whether a 'Gillick-competent' child should be able to override the lack of parental consent and whether the consent of one parent should be sufficient for the participation of a non-Gillick competent child. The trainers' group took the view that both parents' consent should be a precondition for children's participation in mediation, because lack of parental consent would be likely to result in the parents abandoning mediation or refusing to consider their child's messages. Children and young people would be placed in a very difficult position in talking with a mediator against the wishes of one or both parents. If the views and wishes they express are dismissed by their parents, they are likely to feel even more rejected.

2 Confidentiality

Conversations with a child or young person in mediation are confidential and not reportable to the court or to third parties, except where there are safeguarding and child protection concerns, or in exceptional circumstances where the court imposes an overriding obligation of disclosure upon the mediator. The child or young person may give the mediator permission to share their messages and suggestions with their parents, but the child's words are not reportable to the court by the mediator. The confidentiality of conversations with children in mediation is more complicated than gaining consent, because different aspects need careful attention: a) safeguarding a child at risk; b) confidentiality in relation to the family justice system; and c) the mediator's responsibilities towards and for the child.

(a) Safeguarding

Mediators must check carefully at initial meetings and throughout mediation for different forms and levels of abuse and for any concerns about a child's safety and well-being. Mediators must be alert to any indications of harm or risks concerning the psychological and emotional, as well as physical, safety of children. 'The protection of children from risk of physical and emotional abuse must always take precedence in any "best interests" consideration.'[19] Where a participant indicates concerns, the mediator must enquire whether these concerns have been reported and if so, when, by whom and to whom, and whether a child protection service

19 Bryant, D, Chief Justice of the Family Court of Australia, *An Australian perspective on the Family Justice Review*, International Family Law Lecture, London 2012, 24.

is currently involved. Wherever there are indications that a child is, or may be, at risk of harm, the mediator must contact the duty social worker immediately.[20] However, it needs to be borne in mind that, in some cases, insufficient grounds may be found to warrant a protection order or other preventive action. The child's right to be heard is not invariably upheld and even when the child is heard by those working in child protection, the child's words may be disregarded.[21]

SAFEGUARDING THE CHILD IN CASES INVOLVING CHILD SEXUAL ABUSE

Statutory guidance on safeguarding children and on inter-agency work to safeguard and promote the welfare of children was updated in February 2019.[22] Since then, rates of domestic and child abuse have shown a sharp increase, particularly during the Covid-19 pandemic and periods of lockdown. Over the last six years, there has been a 57% increase in reported cases of child sexual abuse, a rate which the Centre of Expertise on Child Sexual Abuse attributes in large part to greater awareness and more willingness to report offences.[23] Child sexual abuse may be perpetrated by a sibling, generally by an older brother abusing a younger sister.[24] The abused child may not tell anyone, fearing the consequences of doing so. The Report of the Independent Inquiry on Child Sexual Abuse has also raised concerns over the scale of child abuse in unregistered schools and groups run by religious groups of all denominations.[25] The Centre of Expertise on Child Sexual Abuse has published guidelines on talking with children who have experienced sexual abuse.[26] The Centre also provides training for social workers, teachers and the police to increase awareness of child sexual abuse and skills in detecting signals from a distressed child.

Empathy and skills are needed to pick up indications from a child's body language and to ask sensitively worded questions. Parents may express concerns about a child's well-being that do not require a safeguarding check, but which indicate a need for medical, therapeutic or other help. Mediators should provide information about helping agencies, websites and other resources and signpost parents to mental health services. It may be very difficult, however, to access these services, because, like many other public services, they are insufficiently staffed and funded. Researchers at the University of Exeter have recommended that each school should have a member of staff trained in mental health support for children and young people.[27]

---

20 FMC Code of Practice for Family Mediation 2018, 5.5.3.

21 See Ch 8 on allegations of 'parental alienation' and children's reports of domestic abuse.

22 *Working Together to Safeguard Children* (DfE 2018); *Statutory guidance on inter-agency working to safeguard and promote the welfare of children* (DfE 2015, updated February 2019).

23 Centre of Expertise on Child Sexual Abuse, BBC News, 28 July 2023.

24 Yates, P and Allardyce, S, *Sibling sexual abuse – A Knowledge and Practice Overview*, Centre of Expertise on Child Sexual Abuse, January 2021.

25 Independent Inquiry on Child Sexual Abuse Child Protection in Religious Organisations and Settings Report, September 2021.

26 www.csacentre.org.uk/knowledge-in-practice/practice-improvement/communicating-with-children-guide/.

27 See n 14 and Ch 10

(b) Confidentiality in relation to court proceedings

A mediator's conversation with a child or young person is legally privileged and is not reportable to the court or to third parties, except, as explained above, where there are safeguarding concerns or where, in exceptional circumstances, the law imposes an overriding obligation of disclosure on the mediator. A judge could find an overriding obligation in law that would allow the cloak of confidentiality to be lifted in certain circumstances. In the case of *Re J (A Child: Disclosure)*,[28] the Court of Appeal was faced with the dilemma of respecting a child's confidentiality while also providing justice to a parent. The court observed that the stakes were high on both sides of the equation and decided that the balance was in favour of disclosing information from the child. Mediators need to be aware, therefore, that in exceptional circumstances they could be called on to testify in court.[29] However, in a more recent Hague Convention case, the judge said he wished to reassure mediators that, except where there is risk of significant harm to a child, 'the cloak of confidentiality remains as securely fastened as ever it was'.[30]

It may be helpful to draw a distinction between the confidentiality of the *content* of what a child says to the mediator and the *fact* that the child has spoken with a mediator. When terms of settlement are worked out in mediation, the mediator's Summary of Proposals is confidential and is not reportable to the court. However, with both participants' written consent, preferably after taking independent legal advice, the Mediation Summary may be made available to the court to facilitate the making of a consent order. A Summary that is made available to the court may refer to the *fact* that the child or young person talked with the mediator and that the child's views and wishes were taken into account by their parents, but the Summary must not report the *content* of what the child said to the mediator.

(c) Confidentiality for the child/young person

It must be explained to the child that where there are any indications of a child being at risk of significant harm, these concerns must be reported to a child protection service. Children understand this exception to confidentiality and generally know it already from their teachers. Unless there are concerns of this kind, children welcome the opportunity to talk with the mediator in confidence, with the assurance that the mediator will not report what they say to the court or to third parties and that their messages and suggestions will be shared with their parents only at their request. Children and young people welcome the opportunity to talk freely and to be able to decide themselves the content of a message or suggestion that they ask the mediator to share with their parents.[31] The mediator shares their messages, without adding interpretations, opinions or advice. The trainers' group sought the views of the Family Justice Young People's Board (FJYPB) on their proposed policy on confidentiality. A member of the FJYPB said: 'I especially like the emphasis on parents or guardians not being able to ask children what was discussed or tell them to say anything because I think that's very important.'

---

28 [2012] EWCA Civ 1204.
29 Ramsay, LJ. *Farm Assist v Defra* [2009] EWHC 1102 (TCC).
30 *BL v TC and LD* [2017] EWHC 3363.
31 See comments from young people in Chs 6 and 12.

There are some circumstances, however, in which a mediator could be placed in a dilemma. For example, a child could confide a 'secret' that does not involve abuse or risk of serious harm, but which could give rise to concern that carrying this 'secret' is putting excessive emotional and psychological pressure on the child. What steps can the mediator take to lift an oppressive secret from a child's shoulders, without breaching the child's confidentiality and betraying their trust? When faced with a dilemma of this kind, the mediator should consult their professional practice consultant (PPC), who must also be qualified in talking with children, to explore the situation further and clarify their course of action. Ongoing specific training in conversations with children and case discussions with colleagues are also essential.

3 Impartiality of the mediator

Mediators must maintain their impartiality in talking with a child or young person and remain neutral regarding the outcome of the mediation, except where a child might be put at risk of harm. The mediator's role is to facilitate communication and encourage co-operation between family members, without acting as the child's advocate or representative and without becoming aligned either with a parent or with a child. The mediator should not give advice, express opinions, or steer the participants towards an outcome favoured by the mediator. There can be situations, as indicated above, where a mediator has difficulty remaining detached when talking with a distressed child or young person in need of help. To avoid over-involvement and to maintain sufficient professional distance, the mediator should turn to their PPC for support and guidance.

4 Decisions rest with the child's parents/those holding parental responsibility

Mediators must take care not to raise a child's hopes of achieving the solution they are hoping for, or to feel in any way responsible for the outcome. Children and young people may make requests and offer suggestions, but they are not asked to make choices and they do not carry responsibility for decisions. They should be reassured by the mediator that their parents have promised not to question or reproach them about what they said, or did not say, to the mediator and they should not feel in any way responsible for the outcome. Their parents or guardians are encouraged to take account of their children's views and suggestions in reaching their decisions, not only because children are autonomous family members who are entitled to express their views, but also because decisions that take account of children's views and suggestions are more likely to be sustained in practice. The goal is not to undermine parents' decisions, but to strengthen them through understanding their children's feelings and concerns.

The core principles outlined in this chapter provide a strong foundation for mediators' training and practice in talking with children and young people. The following chapter describes the regulation of training and practice through the introduction of national requirements for child-inclusive mediation.

Chapter 3

Requirements for child-inclusive mediators and trainers

Family mediators who talk with children have a distinct role that calls for specific additional training, irrespective of their previous qualifications and experience. Personal qualities are important, not only knowledge and skills. As previously emphasised, mediators need warmth and empathy to engage with children and gain their trust. Sensitivity and patience are needed to reach those who are shy and anxious, while a direct and open manner helps to connect with disillusioned teenagers who may consider adults a waste of time, having been let down too often. Children and young people need to be respected as equals, with their own individuality and point of view. If they are talked down to and patronised, they will simply switch off.

Introducing requirements for child-inclusive mediation

The recommendations put forward by the trainers' group in May 2017 for mediators' training to talk with young people, pre-requisites and continuing professional development were accepted in full by the Family Mediation Council (FMC) and the Mediation Standards Board (FMSB). The FMC took immediate steps to implement these recommendations by issuing transitional requirements for all mediators to meet by the end of December 2018. Mediators not previously trained in child-inclusive mediation (ChiM)[1] were required to attend an Awareness and Understanding Day to gain more understanding of the process, its objectives and principles, different ways of including children and young people and pre-requisites for doing so. Mediators who attended these Awareness and Understanding days gave very positive feedback, saying they had gained more understanding and felt better equipped to provide information to parents. Many said that they wanted to train in ChiM when they became accredited. Mediators who were already trained in ChiM were required to attend an Update Day provided by trainers approved by the FMC. These training days produced a significantly higher take-up of ChiM. The FMC reported that the proportion of children aged ten and over who talked with a mediator nearly doubled from 14% in 2017 to 26% in 2019.[2] Attendance at a one-day ChiM introductory course is now a requirement for accreditation and thus for acceptance for ChiM training, providing a bridge to the further understanding and competencies needed for this specialised area of work.

1 The acronym ChiM (Children in Mediation) is used from here onwards, in preference to CIM (see Foreword).

2 www.familymediationcouncil.org.uk/wp-content/uploads/2020/01/Family-Mediation-Survey-Autumn-2019-Results.pdf.

Additions to the FMC Code of Practice for Mediators

Requirements for mediators' training and practice were introduced in new clauses inserted in the FMC Code of Practice, reissued in 2018. An additional clause inserted in the section on 'Welfare of children' states that: 'The Mediator must encourage the Participants to consider the children's wishes and feelings. All children and young people aged 10 and above should be offered the opportunity to have their voices heard directly during the mediation, if they wish.'[3] The section of the Code on Qualifications and Training includes a clause stating that: 'Mediators may undertake child-inclusive Mediation only when they: (a) have registered to do so with the FMC; and (b) have met the requirements as may be laid down by the FMC.'[4]

The Exeter researchers commented that the FMC's revised Code of Practice made only brief references to child-inclusive mediation. In their policy recommendations following a study of children's participation in mediation, the researchers called for a specific Code of Practice covering mediators' training and practice in this field of work. 'We suggest that now is the time to develop a code specifically for those engaging in CIM (child-inclusive mediation), with requirements for CPD.'[5] ChiM mediators have requested the FMC to issue a Code of Practice for ChiM training and practice. In the meantime, a draft Code is included at Appendix B.

The FMC Manual of Professional Standards and Regulatory Framework[6] states that:

> 'all mediators should explain to parents/carers at initial information and assessment meetings, as well as subsequently, that children and young people aged 10 and above should have the opportunity to have a conversation with a professionally qualified mediator or child consultant in which they are invited to give their perspective, in order that parents may take account of those perspectives in any decisions or arrangements that are being made for them'.

Exceptions include safeguarding concerns, or where a child has learning difficulties or mental illness that make their participation inappropriate. Both parents/carers must sign the Agreement to Mediate and give their written consent to their child's participation. If the child has a parent or legal guardian who is not a participant in the mediation, their consent should be sought as well.

Requirements for ChiM trainers

Trainers wishing to provide ChiM training are required to submit their training programme to the FMC and Standards Board for approval, with full details of the syllabus and training methods. Courses must run with sufficient participants to support skills development, with a maximum number so that trainers can assess the competency of each mediator in role-plays and exercises. Courses must have

3 Family Mediation Council Code of Practice revised 2018, para 6.6.1.
4 Ibid.
5 University of Exeter Wellcome Centre, Healthy Relationships Project, *Report and Key Findings* (wcceh.org), March 2022, Policy Implications, 15.
6 FMC-Manual-of-Professonal-Standards-Regulatory-Framework-v1.3-Updated-June-2019, Part 6.

a minimum of one core trainer for every six participants. The trainers' group recommended that training in child-inclusive mediation should provide at least 40 hours of learning and development, 19 hours of which may consist of designated pre-course reading, pre-course assignments, discussion with a professional practice consultant (PPC) qualified in ChiM, and a post-course assignment. The other 21 hours (equating to three days of training, seven hours per day), 'must be provided in a directly attended course in which at least 50% of the time is spent on skills development, including role-play and small group exercises'. These requirements were approved by the FMC and are included in the FMC's Standards Framework.[7] At the time, it did not occur to the trainers' group that a 'directly attended course' could be interpreted as attended online, as online training hardly existed at that time. However, training online has become widely available, largely in response to the Covid-19 pandemic. Some training providers now offer ChiM training online, but this is an unsatisfactory substitute for attendance at an 'in person' course and taking part in role-plays in which body language can be observed, as well as verbal communication, with participants giving feedback and discussing with each other freely and spontaneously. The FMC has been asked to review the requirements for training providers and make them more explicit.

The trainers' group recommended that training courses should cover knowledge and performance requirements, with opportunities for participants to take part in simulated child inclusive mediation/s and produce documents, such as drafting invitations to children and young people and documents to record parental agreement.[8] ChiM training needs to include a range of methods to help mediators develop skills and apply their knowledge in practice. Role-plays are particularly important, because mediators taking the roles of parents or children can gain new insights, while those taking the role of mediator are faced with 'real life' situations in which they need to respond quickly and empathetically, managing conflicts and power imbalances, exploring options and asking questions that help participants to look to the future, rather than back to the past.

The trainers' group drew up a list of competencies (areas of knowledge and 'performance skills') that mediators need to demonstrate in order to be qualified to talk with children and young people in mediation. These are listed in Section 6 of the FMC Manual of Professional Standards and Self-Regulatory Framework.[9]

Requirements for applicants for ChiM training

The ChiM trainers' group recommended to the FMC that a mediator wishing to apply for training must: a) be currently registered with the FMC as a fully accredited mediator; b) have completed a minimum number of child-related mediations; and c) have the written support of their professional practice consultant (PPC), together with any further confirmation requested by the trainers. The ChiM trainers' recommendations were accepted by the FMC and the Family Mediation Standards Board at the end of May 2017 and new requirements and standards for ChiM training and practice were issued for all mediators on the FMC Register.

7 FMC Professional Standards and Self-Regulatory Framework, 47, 6.10b.
8 ChiM trainers' group, Paper 3, para3.3.
9 FMC, www.familymediationcouncil.org.uk/wp-content/uploads/2022/08/FMC-MIAM-Standards-August-2022.pdf.

Requirements for ChiM practice

The ChiM trainers' group drew up a list of pre-requisites for children's participation in mediation. These pre-requisites were accepted by the FMC and included in the Professional Standards and Self-Regulatory Framework.

1. The mediator's role in talking with a child or young person must be clarified with and accepted by parents/carers. Confidentiality and its limits should be explained and parents/carers should understand and accept the principles and objectives of involving the child directly. They should sign a letter confirming their consent and their willingness to receive messages that their child asks the mediator to share with them. The consent form should include undertakings in which parents/carers confirm that they will not coach the child on what the child should say to the mediator (or not say), nor question or reproach the child afterwards about what the child said, or did not say.
2. A mediator who undertakes to talk with children and young people must be specifically trained to do so, having completed a training programme that has been approved by the FMC and having demonstrated the competencies required for recognition as a ChiM-qualified mediator.
3. The mediator must have suitable rooms and facilities where children and young people will be safe at all times and feel comfortable and at ease.
4. The mediator should consider having a co-mediator or colleague who is available to take part in, or observe, a meeting with a child or young person, as a safeguard against the possibility of an allegation being made against the mediator.

Professional practice consultancy

ChiM mediators should discuss their mediations and reflect on learning points with a professional practice consultant (PPC) who must also be ChiM-qualified. The PPC provides support and encourages continuing professional development through reading, group discussions and attendance at further ChiM-specific training days. The trainers' group recommended that ChiM mediators should undertake a minimum of three ChiM cases and at least one day of ongoing ChiM-specific training every three years, in addition to the requirements for all mediators to undertake the necessary hours of continuing professional development, confirmed by their PPC, in order to maintain their FMC registration. Where it is not possible to meet the practice requirement, the mediator should attend refresher training in ChiM to ensure that their practice is up to date and may count this refresher training as part of their ChiM professional development requirement. These recommendations were accepted by the FMC and FMSB and incorporated in the FMC's Standards and Regulatory Framework.[10]

---

10 www.familymediationcouncil.org.uk/wp-content/uploads/2022/05/FMC-Manual-of-Professonal-Standards-Regulatory-Framework-v1.4.1-Updated-1-March-2022.pdf.

Knowledge base for child-inclusive mediation

In talking with parents and children of different ages, mediators need to draw from a wide knowledge base that includes theoretical frameworks, relevant areas of family law and research studies on children's needs in separation and divorce. The knowledge requirements for ChiM training and practice listed in the FMC Standards include:

(a) Family systems theory.

(b) Attachment theory.

(c) Child and adolescent development (physical, cognitive and moral development).

(d) Crisis and resilience theory.

(e) Research on the effects of separation and divorce on children, the significance of their involvement in decision-making and models of ChiM practice.

(f) The potential effect of power imbalances between parents and children in ChiM practice.

(g) The range of communication and behaviours resulting from culture, age, gender, ability, additional needs, racial or religious diversity and how to respond to these.

(h) Relevant law and legislation in private law children's matters and on: a) the child and young person's right to be heard (including Article12 of the United Nations Convention on the Rights of the Child 1989 (UNCRC 1989)); b) equality and inclusion; and c) legislation and statutory requirements on safeguarding and domestic abuse, risk assessment and safeguarding.

Many of these subjects, such as supporting and rebuilding attachments,[11] research on children's experience of separation and divorce,[12] and building resilience[13] are referred to in other chapters in this book.

Continuing professional development in ChiM

The extensive range of knowledge required by ChiM mediators cannot be covered in a short training course. Knowledge needs to be extended in continuing professional development. The trainers' group proposed that ongoing ChiM training may be undertaken in a number of ways, including training courses to develop and update skills and knowledge in specific areas; reading to expand theoretical, legal or practical knowledge; attending a conference workshop or lecture relevant to ChiM theory or practice; writing or delivering new material relevant to ChiM, such as giving a workshop or lecture relevant to ChiM, or writing and publishing an article.

11 See Chs 4 and 8.
12 See Ch 11.
13 See Ch 12.

A family systems perspective

Each family is unique, just as each child is unique, and a family systems perspective helps mediators to understand different family structures and the relationships between children, parents and other family members.[14] Ken Cloke, writing on *Mediation and meditation: the deeper middle way*,[15] suggests that there are two middle ways of helping participants in mediation to resolve their issues and that they have very different outcomes. The first way consists of negotiating between positions and brokering an agreement. The second middle way involves committed listening, open-hearted empathetic dialogue and creative problem-solving. Mediators need to combine the logical, systematic approach of left-brain thinking with right-brain thinking, which encourages creativity and intuition and makes connections holistically.

If mediators focus on issues between separating and divorcing couples, children's interests and wish to be heard may be sidelined. It is also important to recognise the influence of other family members and professional advisers. Mediators need to understand the structure of the particular family, the stage of separation or other major change, and whether relationships between the parents, and between each parent and each child, are close, conflicted, or have broken down. Meetings may involve different constellations of parents, children and other family members. A systems framework also helps to make connections between private decision-making by families, public systems of decision-making and support services, with referrals channelled between them, as recommended by the Family Solutions Group. Families are 'small arcs of larger circles'.[16] Understanding family systems with an 'ecosystemic' perspective helps mediators to navigate complex family dynamics and facilitate connections, not only between family members, but also between the family and support systems.[17]

The design and use of ecograms

To seek an overview of a particular family and reflect on possible ways forward, mediators may find it useful to draw an ecogram. An ecogram shows the structure of the family in a way that distinguishes the couple's relationship, which is ending, from the parental relationship that needs to continue. It is a tool that mediators may draw in their case notes to remind themselves of the family's names and other key information and to stimulate reflection, possibly in discussion with their PPC, about the focus and management of the mediation process. The ecogram may also be drawn on a flip-chart or screen to encourage child-focused discussions with participants in mediation and to stimulate fresh perceptions. Whereas a geneogram depicts a (generally) 'intact' family in vertical, generational lines, an ecogram can show family members and carers in blended families in which children move between different households on a regular or irregular basis. When separated

14 Parkinson, L, *Conciliation in Separation and Divorce* (Croom Helm, 1986), reissued by Routledge, 2023 and *Family Mediation* (4th edn, LexisNexis, 2020).

15 Cloke, K, *Mediation and meditation: the deeper middle way* (2009) mediate.com Weekly No. 266.

16 Bateson, G, *Small Arcs of Larger Circles* (Triarchy Press, 2016).

17 Parkinson, L, 'Ecosystemic family mediation' [2022] *Family Law* 375.

parents acquire new partners, the family grows outwards on a horizontal axis. An ecogram depicts the family landscape (using computer terminology here to mean a wider picture) rather than the family in portrait format (ie, a narrower, linear format).[18] The ecogram uses dotted lines (ie, permeable boundaries) to show movement between households and the interactions between 'old' and 'new' family systems. If the mediator is sketching the ecogram for their own reference, different colours may be used to depict relationships as close, amicable, hostile or broken.

The difficulties of ending a partner relationship while continuing to co-parent need to be acknowledged. The feelings – or threads – of these relationships often become entangled. Separating them out visually in a diagram helps parents to see that the threads of their partnership need to be disentangled from the threads that connect them as parents. A diagram of children held by both parents jointly in a basket-shaped 'container' of love, care and protection can have a powerful effect on parents, especially in the early stages of separation. The mediator may observe that children who continue to enjoy both parents' support feel secure. However, if one parent drops their handle of the basket, the children are liable to fall, even if the other parent holds on to their handle. This observation can make a considerable impact on parents, who can be encouraged that the fact that they are taking part in mediation shows that they are both holding their handle of the 'basket.'

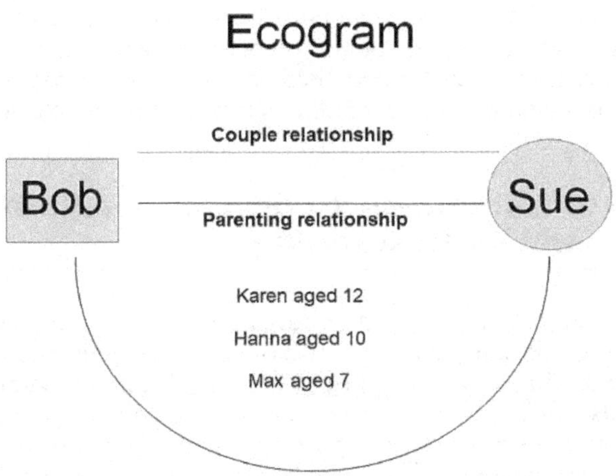

Drawing an ecogram with parents in mediation needs sensitivity and care. For example, it would be insensitive and unhelpful to include a new partner who is seen by the left-behind parent as the cause of the break-up, whereas at a later stage of separation, the role of the new partner may be accepted and usefully discussed. An ecogram showing parents, children and different generations is particularly helpful when the family includes siblings and half-siblings who are moving between parents in different households.

18 Parkinson, L, *Family Mediation* (4th edn, LexisNexis, 2020) 44.

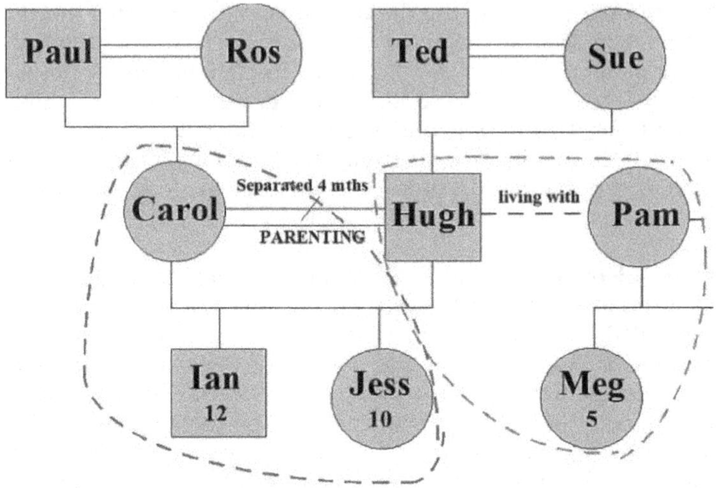

Extending mediators' knowledge and skills without risking overload

Mediators' concerns that involving children directly in mediation may cause distress to a child may serve as a cover for the mediator's own anxieties. The Mapping Paths to Family Justice study[19] found that one of the main barriers to children's participation was mediators' lack of confidence in talking with a child on their own.

A pre-course assignment to develop mediators' confidence and understanding

In a pre-course assignment designed to develop confidence, the mediator is asked to talk with the son or daughter of a friend or colleague, who knows the mediator as a family friend. The family should not be going through separation or divorce. With the parents' consent, the mediator consults the child or young person about what they think would make it easier for others in their age group, whose parents are separating or separated, to talk with a mediator, and what they think would make it harder. The mediator should explain to their consultee that they will not be asked questions about their own family, only their advice on talking with others of a similar age who are experiencing separation or divorce. The consultee is told that the mediator will not share what they say with their parents, but they can of course tell their parents about it if they wish. The mediator may say: 'I'll help you with your homework, if you help me with mine!' and ask permission to share their advice with other mediators, giving the consultee's age and gender, but not their name or identifying details. Mediators who have undertaken this assignment are impressed by the level of understanding, imagination and empathy shown by young people in talking about feelings and reactions that lie outside their own experience, and by the extent to which their views and advice concur. All those

19 Barlow, A, et al, *Mapping Paths to Family Justice – Briefing Paper and Report on Key Findings* (Universities of Exeter and Kent, June 2014).

consulted agree with each other that children should be able to have a say. Some of them are indignant that a child might not be asked. 'Martin', aged 15, said he felt strongly that young people should be consulted and have their views treated with respect. The mediator should provide clear prior explanations and listen, without taking notes. Confidentiality is very important. Provide snacks! It would be better to talk with the same mediator who knows both parents and who is able to share messages directly with them. Martin said that guys don't share things like this with their friends. A boy might feel more comfortable talking with a male mediator, but not necessarily so. The mediator should not be too formal or condescending and should thank the young person for their input.

The following quotes come from consultees, all of whom considered that young people should be consulted about where they want to live and how often they should see their other parent. 'Talking to a mediator would be better than seeing a Judge or having to go to Court.' Mediators need to take care over the way they present themselves and engage with the young person. 'The mediator should be smiley and nice, a friendly mediator, definitely not dressed in a suit but not in jeans, as that would look as if they weren't taking it seriously. Make sure you smile, as a smile can make others smile and feel comfortable. Don't stare at the child. Stress that you are not there to put pressure on them. They may be worried that their parents won't like what they say. You need to stress you definitely won't tell their parents if they don't want you to. REALLY LISTEN. If everything is too serious, you've got to break the pressure. Don't make cheesy jokes or try too hard. 'Don't jump right in, asking lots of questions, without explaining things first, it wouldn't be good.' In another conversation, a brother and sister aged 10 and 12 agreed that the mediator should smile a lot, but not make jokes and not be 'creepishly grinning'. They liked the idea of writing their own message 'because then I would know what's being shown to my parents'. A 14-year-old girl said: 'It would be good to talk to the mediator about things and not to Mum and Dad. If you don't have anyone else to talk to, you bottle things up inside.' Young people recognise that:

> 'it would be hard not knowing the person and going to an office to talk to the mediator. They should not meet somewhere that was boring looking. It should be somewhere they could just sit and talk. It would help if it were colourful and comfortable with bright pictures, beanbags or a sofa. Definitely not at school, as other pupils and friends would wonder why they have been taken out of lessons.'

Some mediators, however, talk with children at school and report that this works well.

One mediator who undertook this assignment had a conversation with 'Emily', aged nine. Emily thought that most children would definitely want to speak to someone about their wishes and feelings and that all children should be offered the opportunity to speak to a grown-up who was not part of their family or friends. Emily thought that the grown-up should reassure the child that they could say what they wanted and that they didn't have tell the grown-up everything, if they didn't want to. The grown-up should not go through a list of questions, they should just let the child talk freely and there should be no direct questions to start with. The child should be able to decide if they would like what they say to be shared with their parents, or nothing shared at all. Emily suggested that when meeting the grown-up, the child should be able to take something that is special to them, for example a teddy bear or blanket. The grown-up should have a 'smiley face and wear nice clothes, seem gentle and look like they can help'. The room should be comfortable, it shouldn't have a computer or a hard desk chair. It should be a happy and cheerful room, with a special seat, such as a comfy armchair and maybe some flowers and pictures on the walls of drawings by other children who have visited. There should be some toys, paper and colouring pencils, so that the child can draw how they are feeling if they don't want to speak about their feelings, and play-doh to help children express how they are feeling. They should be offered a drink and a biscuit or sweets or chocolate and the grown-up should start by explaining that 'I do not have to tell your mum and dad anything, unless you want me to.' The grown-up should explain that 'talking to me might help you to feel better', and the child should be reassured that 'no-one will be cross with what you say and no one will get upset'. Emily felt it was important to reassure the child that he or she is not alone in this situation.

The mediator asked Emily what she thought should be done if there is more than one child in the family. Emily said the grown-up should let the children choose if they want to speak alone, or with their brothers and/or sisters, or a combination of both. Emily commented 'I would be happy to talk to you and I would be happy to share my feelings with you.' She said she was happy to continue talking and seemed to be enjoying herself. She thought some children might have 'jumbled up feelings' that might come out at the wrong time, if they do not speak to someone. She talked about her friend at school whose mum and dad had split up a few years ago and said her friend was really sad. Her friend's brother was not very nice to her and her friend would talk to Emily about what was going on at home. Emily said her friend felt better after talking to her. She offered more ideas and opinions than the mediator had expected from her and following her advice, the mediator decided to make some improvements to the room she currently used, or use another room.

Another mediator talked with a girl aged 17, who had experienced her parents' separation when she was young. Her father had remarried and her stepmother had two daughters from her previous marriage. 'Caroline' said it was very important for young people to be able to offload and be listened to. It was difficult for them to talk to their parents, but parents should take their child's views into account and the child should not take decisions. Parents should review their arrangements regularly and be ready to change them. A child may not like their parent's new partner or their children, and shouldn't be forced, but it was difficult to explain these feelings to the parent and it could cause conflict with the other parent, so it may be easier to for the child to just bottle things up. The child may be grieving. Children should be invited to come, not told to come.

This pre-course assignment has been used in ChiM training in several countries and in each country the mediators reported that they gained valuable advice and insights from their consultees. An Ukrainian family mediator[20] gave an account of her conversation with her friend's two sons, aged 9 and 14. The 9-year-old, living with his brother in a happy and stable family, explained that 'when parents quarrel, their child feels like a wild boar, because a boar can hide in the bushes ('I've seen that'), and the parents are like dogs, because they bark at each other and nothing is heard'. The assurance of confidentiality was important for both boys. The 14-year-old said: 'Okay! Because then I can relax and not think that later my parents will interrogate me and I will have to explain something.' In her concluding comments,

20 Anzhelika Golovchenko, Ukrainian mediator, quoted with consent.

the mediator wrote: 'This exercise gave me a real experience of communicating with children, the opportunity to hear and feel them, and this experience saved me from fear and some confusion in working with children in mediation in parental conflicts.'

Before moving on to the next stage of inviting a child or young person to have a talk with a mediator, there are some other questions to consider, such as the age of the child, differences in culture and ethnicity and to what extent 'child-inclusive mediation' is actually inclusive.

Chapter 4

Diversity and Inclusivity

A number of questions arise in considering whether a child should be invited to talk with a mediator and contribute to decision-making and if so, in what way. Is the model of child-inclusive mediation currently practised in the UK truly inclusive, or does it cater mainly for children in a certain age range from certain kinds of families? The answer seems to be that it is not inclusive for a number of reasons, including financial disadvantage, the age of the child and ethnicity.

Financial disadvantage

Children in low-income families may have no opportunity to talk with a mediator, because the legal aid scheme may be insufficient to cover the costs, even when combined with the voucher scheme. Parents who are just above the legal aid limit may be unable to pay for additional sessions. Successive governments have ignored this injustice to under-privileged children. Public funding should be provided to cover the cost for all children and young people wishing to be heard in mediation. The outlay would be offset by cost savings resulting from higher rates of settlement through mediation, as evidenced by research.[1]

The age of the child

Under the Children Act 1989, the court is required, when making a child arrangements order in private family law proceedings, to have regard to the wishes and feelings of the child concerned. The Act states that seeking the child's views should be considered 'in the light of the child's age and understanding'.[2] A study of public and private law child proceedings commissioned by the Ministry of Justice to inform family justice developments in England and Wales[3] found that the majority of the children who were the subject of proceedings were under ten years old. 76% of children in 393 private law cases were under ten years old, 20% were under two years old and a further 18% were under four years old. Some may assume that children under ten years old are too young to be competent to express their views on arrangements that will affect them in the longer term. Morrow[4] found, however, that even young children can understand and talk about the notion of being listened to and that most children wanted a say in matters affecting them. In

1 See Chs 11 and 12
2 Children Act 1989, s 1.
3 Cassidy and Davey, Ministry of Justice Research Summary 2011, 5/11.
4 Morrow, V, 'Children's Perspectives on Families' 1998 *Joseph Rowntree Research Findings* 798.

her study of children's mental capacities, Donaldson[5] found that, provided children receive care and support, they can be skilled in thinking and using language by the time they start primary school. In a large-scale study involving a sample of 467 children aged from 5 to 16, Dunn and Deater-Deckard found that children as young as five could express their views through maps and pictures and that their views chimed with those expressed by older children.[6] Childline found from their experience of phone calls from children that 'children are perfectly able to enter into discussions about the future, as long as they are not asked to choose in an atmosphere of acute conflict where they feel caught in the middle'.[7]

The Children Act and the UN Convention on the Rights of the Child 1989 call for the child's age and maturity to be taken into account, without specifying an age limit. State signatories to the Convention were advised by the UN Committee on the Rights of the Child that they should not set age limits, either in law or practice, that would restrict the child's right to be heard.[8] The UK College Policy and Practice Guidelines on Children, Young People and Family Mediation[9] advised that, in deciding whether, when and how children should be directly consulted in mediation, full consideration should be given to many aspects, including 'a checklist for determining the kinds of circumstances when direct consultation might or might not be appropriate, the range of possible options and models for consultation, the culture, religion and ethnicity of the family, the developmental stage of each child and the emotional and psychological state of each child'. The Guidelines did not stipulate an age range for children's participation and the FMC Code of Practice 2010 followed the Guidelines in stating that:

> 'at all times mediators must have special regard to the welfare of any children of the family. They should encourage participants to focus on the needs and interests of the children as well as on their own. Mediators must encourage participants to consider the children's wishes and feelings. If appropriate, they may discuss with them whether and to what extent it is proper to consult the children directly in order to ascertain their wishes and feelings. Where mediators and both participants agree that it is appropriate to consult any children directly, the consent of the children must first be obtained. Mediators consulting directly with any children must have been specifically trained to do so.'[10]

The Voice of the Child Dispute Resolution Advisory Group considered that 'age and maturity are not relevant in determining whether a child should be heard. They become relevant only with regard to how much weight to attach to the child's views'.[11] Their Final Report in 2015 took a different position, however, stating their aim of 'embedding a changing culture where the voice of the children within mediation will become the norm (for children aged 10 and over)'.[12] The FMC revised Code of Practice issued in September 2016 adopted this age range in an additional clause stating that 'All children and young people aged 10 and

5 Donaldson, M, *Children's Minds* (Fontana Press, 1987).
6 Dunn, J and Deater-Deckard, K, 'Children's views of their changing families' 2001 *Joseph Rowntree Research findings* 931.
7 Childline Report, Unhappy Parents, Unhappy Children, 1998.
8 UN Committee on the Rights of the Child, 1 July 2009, 21.
9 UK College of Family Mediators, Children, Young People and Family Mediation – Policy and Practice Guidelines 2000, see also Ch 2.
10 FMC Code of Practice 2010, s 5.7.
11 Voice of the Child Group, Draft Policy and Practice Guidelines, January 2015, Appx 1 iii.
12 Voice of the Child Group Final Report, 2015, Introduction.

above should be offered the opportunity to have their voices heard directly during the Mediation, if they wish.'[13] The FMC Manual of Professional Standards and Regulatory Framework[14] makes it clear that 'younger children (including younger siblings and other children of the family) should not be excluded from having a similar opportunity, since they are equally important members of the family'.

Children mature at different rates and their ability to express their views and wishes is affected by many factors, including family culture and circumstances and the individual child's personality and confidence. The Department of Health advised in 2004 that children as young as three should be consulted about their care when in hospital. Doctors and nurses were advised that they should not only consult the parents, but should involve the child as well. Gill Brook, head of child and family-centred care at Birmingham Children's Hospital, said: 'Giving choice to children is about upholding the rights of any human being. We are not talking about making life-saving decisions ... it is really about empowering patients, helping them to learn ... how treatments work.'[15] The UN Committee on the Rights of the Child emphasised that recognition of a child as a holder of rights 'is anchored in a child's daily life from the earliest stage'.[16] Children are capable of forming views at an early age, although they may be unable to express their views verbally.[17] Full implementation of Article 12 of the United Nations Convention on the Rights of the Child 1989 (UNCRC 1989) requires recognition of, and respect for, non-verbal forms of communication including play, facial expressions, and drawing and painting, through which young children can express their feelings, views and dreams. Mediators are encouraged to provide things for children to fiddle with and paper and coloured pens, so that they can doodle while they talk, or draw a picture that the mediator can show their parents. However, unless the mediator is trained in play therapy, mediators should not use play techniques to understand children's feelings and give feedback to parents based on interpreting their child's play.

When children come to talk with the mediator, younger siblings should therefore be invited too, and included in the welcome and introductions. It should not be assumed that they will not want to speak to the mediator on their own. A six-year-old boy said firmly: 'I want my meeting too.' Researchers in Argentina have recounted how an eight-year-old boy knocked on the door of the room in which his parents were meeting with the mediators and complained: 'Nobody asks me anything!'[18] The mediators invited him to join the meeting and explained to him the arrangements that his parents had just worked out together. The boy said he agreed with the arrangements. He was asked to sign the mediation summary, together with his parents, and showed his pleasure in being treated with respect and equal regard.

Young children understand far more than their parents may realise. Even pre-verbal children need explanations of what is happening in calm and reassuring voices. They may not understand all the words, but they hear the reassurance that they

---

13 FMC Code of Practice September 2016, s 5.7.2.
14 FMC Professional Standards and Self-Regulatory Framework updated 2019 Part 6.
15 *The Independent* newspaper, ParentScope, 12 January 2004.
16 UN Committee on the Rights of the Child, 1 July 2009
17 Lansdown, G, *The evolving capacities of the child* (Innocenti Research Centre, UNICEF/Save the Children, Florence 2005).
18 Elstein, S and Felibert, M, 'La Escucha de los Niños en Mediación' May 2023 *La Trama journal*, Argentina.

will always be loved and cared for and that their parents' separation is in no way their fault. They need to feel what Judith Wallerstein calls 'emotional permission' from each parent to continue to love the other parent. Parents may be encouraged to show this 'emotional permission' in a mediation meeting by gently passing their baby or infant from one parent's arms to the other parent's arms. Parents of a young child who agree arrangements for their child in mediation, having argued and possibly shouted at each other in the child's presence, may be invited to come to a final meeting with their child in order to explain their agreement and arrangements to the child. The experience of seeing both parents together in a calm atmosphere and being handed gently between them can be deeply reassuring and calm the child's anxieties.

Children of all ages should have the opportunity to take part in mediation in some way, not only when they are very young, but also as young adults.

Young adults

Young people over 16 may not be invited to talk with a mediator on their own, because they are no longer subject to a child arrangements order and are able to make their own decisions. But they may need the opportunity to talk about their reactions to their parents' separation and how to manage pressure from a parent or resist being drawn into parental arguments. If they are living away at college or university, their parents may assume that they are not greatly affected by their separation. However, college students need a home to come back to in vacations and they may be dependent on financial support from their parents. Many young adults worry about their parents' well being when they are away from home and parenting roles are sometimes reversed. Parents may turn to their children for emotional support and sometimes they need their child as a care-taker. A young person may take on responsibility for looking after a parent who is unwell or disabled. Taking care of an emotionally and/or physically dependent parent brings a burden of responsibility that makes it very difficult for the young person to live their own life. Young adults do not need parents' consent to talk to a mediator, but mediators should mention to parents that they would be glad to have a chat with them, even if everything seems to be going well.

Emma, aged 17, whose parents were just completing their mediation, accepted an invitation to have a chat with the mediator. Her 15-year-old brother, Marlon, also accepted and the mediator met with each of them separately. When Emma arrived, she sat down and began to talk without hesitation:

> 'Well, I need to talk about my relationships with the men in my life (deep breath). First, there's my birth father. I've never met him, but I know his address in London and I feel I'm ready now to contact him and ask him if he would like to meet me. I hope he will agree to meet me. (Another deep breath). Then there's my stepfather. I've been angry with him because we're moving house and I found out he was intending to sell my bed. I'm very attached to my bed and I told him he has no right to sell it without asking me. I think he's keeping the bed now and I need to make my peace with him. (Another deep breath). Then there's my brother. He and I have been arguing and fighting and we tell tales about each other to our mum, the way we used to do when we were little. This is ridiculous and it has to stop. I know he's having a hard time and I'm going

to support him more. (Another deep breath). Well, that's been REALLY helpful. Thank you SO much.'

Emma gave a beaming smile and said goodbye. The mediator had listened with keen interest and empathy and had barely said a word. Emma needed a sounding-board to think through the steps she planned to take and it helped her that the mediator knew her mother and stepfather and her family situation. Her younger brother, Marlon, talked with the mediator about things he needed to explain to his mother, so that she would not press him to go out with her and her new partner, if he did not want to. He also decided that, rather than refusing his stepfather's suggestion to go out for a walk with him on a Sunday morning, he would explain that he would prefer to go out later in the day, because 'mornings are not my best time.'

Ethnic diversity

Participants in mediation come from diverse cultures and mediators meet with different constellations of family members. The 2021 Census recorded that 10.1% of households in England and Wales contained members who identified with two or more ethnic groups, an increase from 8.7% in 2011. Ethnic groups comprise many smaller groups, each of which may have their own cultural and religious traditions and speak their own language. Mediators need to take care to avoid making assumptions about any particular group or community. Those who work with ethnic minority and mixed-race families need to show their awareness of, and respect for, different cultural traditions and values and develop a range of intervention strategies and skills that are appropriate, relevant and sensitive to diverse groups.[19] The mediator's limited knowledge of each culture needs to be checked out and extended.

Dr Mohamed Keshavjee has trained Ismaili family mediators in around 20 countries worldwide and has written widely on mediation with Muslim communities. Dr Keshavjee observes that 'a Western, individualistic, problem-solving model of mediation ... [is] not totally suitable for a communitarian culture to which most of the Ismaili communities belong'.[20] Professionally qualified Black and Asian mediators are needed who may be accepted more readily by families of similar ethnicity. Mediators from other backgrounds need to understand and take account of 'the complexity of issues that diasporic Muslim communities in Britain have faced, and are still facing'. Dr Keshavjee explains that 'it is possible to interpret the rules of the Sharia to find resonance with basic ADR norms and to use them positively to construct the necessary bridge between Islamic religious law and the laws of the Western countries in which Muslims have settled'.[21]

In mediating with couples from ethnic groups that differ from the mediator's own background, the mediator needs to be aware of cultural norms that may restrict the couple's ability to negotiate freely in mediation, without deferring to the views and approval of senior family members or community leaders. Married couples may be

19 Robinson, L, Cross-cultural child development for social workers – an introduction (Palgrave, 2007).
20 Keshavjee, M, Islam, Sharia and Alternative Dispute Resolution (I.B. Tauris, 2013).
21 ibid 165.

expected to defer to their elders and conflict between a married couple may be treated as a private family matter, with the elders of the family mediating informally between the couple. The couple's parents and the couple themselves may seek guidance from religious leaders, such as Muslim scholars and Imams, rabbis and pastors, who may arrange private meetings to assist the couple to resolve their differences. The couple's personal needs and concerns may be suppressed in collective cultures, where the elders of the family or community may urge the couple to remain together. A reconciliation may be achieved, but problems may continue and if divorce takes place, tensions between the couple and between the couple and their extended families may continue for many years.

Mediators also need to be aware of cultural traditions and values with regard to childcare responsibilities. Summera Kauser, a Muslim family mediator, explains that the cultural norm of assisting one another is highly valued in South Asian communities.[22] Assistance is provided in many ways, including lending money and looking after children on a temporary or permanent basis. Children are brought up by relatives if their parents are unable to look after them. Members of extended families are expected to support each other when they need help. Mediators, including those who share the same ethnicity as both participants, need to appreciate each family's unique history, values and relationships in the context of their cultural and ethnic traditions, without applying our own norms and values, consciously or unconsciously.

Social isolation

A study on *Parenting in Multi-Racial Britain* reported that 'although minority communities reported good frequent contact with their wider family network, the non-availability of some family members, such as grandparents, was of concern to others'.[23] Individuals who migrate to the UK from another country may have experienced trauma and high levels of stress. If they do not have family members to welcome them, they can be in acute need and isolated, especially if couples separate from each other. In some cultures, separation and divorce carry a stigma and a divorced woman may be ostracised. In her book, *Antigona and Me,*[24] Kate Clanchy recounts her friendship with a Kosovan woman whom she meets one day in London. Antigona fears rejection, because she is divorced. 'I am dee-vorced', she says, and looks closely at me, scanning my face for disapproval. 'Dee-vorced. He beat me up.'

There may be urgent need for assistance in situations involving domestic abuse.[25] Keshavjee reports that domestic abuse is prevalent, but often hidden in cultures where a woman avoids reporting it for fear of besmirching the family name. Keshavjee's study found that men may also be victims of domestic abuse and that agencies tend to avoid these issues for fear of making the victim more vulnerable. The relative social isolation of the parent they live with inevitably has an impact on the children. Separating couples need information about services offering assistance and financial advice, but members of some ethnic minority groups may not know

---

22 Kauser, S, 'Mediation and Cultural Diversity' [2022] *Family Law* 1557-61.
23 Barn, R, et al., *Parenting in Multi-Racial Britain* (National Children's Bureau and Joseph Rowntree Foundation, July 2006).
24 Clanchy, K. *Antigona and Me* (Picador, 2008).
25 See Ch 2, Screening for domestic abuse and Safeguarding.

where to turn outside their community. They may lack awareness of mediation as an option. Mediators should enquire at information and assessment meetings whether the individual has support and ask who lives in the same household, in order to build up a picture of family relationships and living arrangements. In explaining the opportunity for children to be included, mediators need to be aware that members of some ethnic groups may feel anxious about the prospect of their child speaking to a mediator from a different culture. Mediators should take extra care to understand cultural differences that may feed into these anxieties.

Linkworker Projects

London and other cities in the UK benefit from their rich diversity of cultures, but if a minority community is segregated from mainstream society, bridges are needed to facilitate social inclusion and provide links to local and national services and institutions. Manchester City Council's commitment to promote integration and inclusion for all residents led to the launch in 1992 of the Linkworker Advice Service, with nine staff recruited from Asian and African communities.[26] Additional funding was obtained in 1995 to meet the needs of the growing refugee population from Somalian, Arabic and Vietnamese communities. Male and female Linkworkers speak a total of 15 different languages and produce translated material targeting specific communities and needs. Talks are given to community groups to ensure that information and explanations of basic rights to support reach as wide an audience as possible. Linkworkers work in partnership with ethnic community groups and with other voluntary organisations to improve Manchester City Council's public sector services. Family mediation services in the Manchester area need to be linked into this hub and translated material needs to be available on the English legal system and conflict resolution services, to provide information and support for separated parents and their children.

Children in ethnic minority and mixed-race families

Non-parental care-taking is common in many cultures and more studies are needed to understand how infant attachments may be formed through a network of attachments, rather than with the dyad of mother and father. In some African communities, children spend much of their time in the care of other adults or older children while the mother is out working. Researchers have suggested that this pattern of child-rearing helps children to develop social skills early in life which leads to better adjustment in social situations later on.[27] In Japan, on the other hand, a study found that mothers are rarely separated from their infants and spend much of their time talking to them and touching them. Consequently, Japanese babies are more distressed by separation from their mother or by the presence of a stranger.[28] Mediators need to be aware that our views on attachment and the

26 Partnership for Multi-Ethnic Inclusion, *Social Linkworking and Inter-Cultural Mediation in Europe* (eds. Molina et al), PfMI, Sweden 2001.

27 Tronick, EZ, et al., 'The Efe Forager Infant and Toddler Patterns of of Social Relationships – Multiple and Simultaneous' (1992) 28 *Journal of Developmental Psychology* 568–577.

28 Miyake, K. et al., 'Infant Temperament, Mothers' Mode of Interaction, and Attachment in Japan' (1985) 50 *Monographs of the Society for Research in Child Development* 276–297.

process by which attachment occurs may be qualitative judgments formed from the perspective of our own culture.[29]

The UN Committee on the Rights of the Child has stated that ethnic minority and migrant children and children who do not speak the majority language have the same rights as other children to express their views and be heard.[30] However, for reasons referred to above, ethnic minority children may not have an equal opportunity to talk with a qualified family mediator. In considering with ethnic minority or mixed-race parents the possibility of including their children in mediation, it is helpful to begin, as in any mediation concerning children, by asking the parents to describe each of their children and talk about their personality, development, performance at school and what the child likes doing. In a mediation with a white British mother and black Jamaican father seeking contact with his nine-year-old son, the father complained that the mother had been trying to exclude him. They were asked if they had a photo of their son. Both parents proudly showed their photos of a good-looking boy who looked very like his father, with the same beaming smile. They both smiled when the mediator remarked on the boy's wide smile. The mother said that her son was keen on cricket, and as his father was also a keen cricketer, they agreed that he would take their son to a cricket match at the weekend. The father also took up the suggestion to borrow a library book about Jamaica and look at it with his son, to help him feel proud of his heritage and learn more about it. Many children have ancestral roots in countries they may never visit.

In another mediation,[31] the mother was a practising Muslim and the father a practising Catholic. Prior to the mediation referral, their 14-year-old son had written to solicitors and the court to ask for a variation in the Child Arrangement Order which stipulated that the children should celebrate Catholic religious holidays with their father and Islamic religious holidays with their mother. The 14-year-old considered that his voice and wishes were not being heard and that he was old enough to make a decision about which religion he wished to follow. He told the mediators that he wished to follow the Islamic faith in his mother's home and no longer wished to attend Christian celebrations with his father. His ten-year-old sister also talked with the mediators but she did not wish anything she said to be shared with her parents. The father was very disappointed by his son's message and needed time to reflect, but following four mediation sessions, the parents agreed to support their son's wishes. They thanked the mediators for listening to their children and said that this had enabled all of them to move forward with greater openness and understanding.

Children from different ethnic backgrounds with varying life experiences develop competencies in language and self-expression at different ages. Opportunities for their participation should be planned according to their culture, life experience and family values.[32] Mediators always need to bear in mind that from a safeguarding perspective, a child can be at risk of abuse from a parent or older sibling, or from a member of the extended family living in the same household.[33] Black and

29 See Ch 8 on Attachment.

30 UN Committee on the Rights of the Child, 1 July 2009, 7.

31 Recounted by Carlie Norris, family mediator, and quoted with thanks.

32 Lansdown, G, *The evolving capacities of the child* (Innocenti Research Centre, UNICEF/Save the Children, Florence 2005).

33 Ministry of Justice (2020) Assessing Risk of Harm to Children and Parents in Private Law Children Cases: Implementation Plan.

mixed race children who report experiencing racial abuse are in great need of support services, both at school and at home. The writer, Caleb Azumah Nelson, a second-generation British Ghanaian with a family split between south London and Accra, went to a local state primary school and won a scholarship to the fee-paying Alleyn's school in Dulwich. Caleb recalled in an interview that he was one of only four Black students in his year. 'Kids can be really wonderful ... and also, really cruel. They don't always understand when they're being cruel ... something that seems an everyday thing to them can be hurtful, slanted.'[34] Children may not realise that they are being abusive, and a white British teacher may not recognise abuse 'under the radar' in school. A study at Durham University's evidence centre for education found a wide gap in acceptance rates for teacher training, based on ethnicity. Minority ethnic applicants were substantially less likely to be accepted, with applicants recorded as Black having the lowest level of acceptance.

Children need information on how to access help and different ways in which they can express their views on matters that concern them. Information about sources of support for children and young people should be provided in medical centres and taught in school in personal, social and health education (PSHE). The Family Solutions sub-group that led on services for children collaborated with the Mapping Paths researchers at Exeter University in designing lesson plans for PSHE classes on young people's rights under Article 12 of the UN Convention on the Rights of the Child.[35] These lesson plans have received prestigious quality mark approval from the PSHE Association and from the Association of Citizen Teaching.[36] Online resources for PSHE teachers are also provided by the Thomas Coram Foundation, which, according to their latest report, reaches 575,000 children in over 2,500 schools.[37] Coram's Life Education Resources help teachers to go beyond the curriculum to help children understand, explain and regulate their emotions. The resources also help children to learn how to navigate risk, how to stay safe on and offline, and how to develop healthy relationships that strengthen them in adolescence and adulthood.

Ongoing work to inform children of their rights and how to access help

In March 2020, the Second Report of the Private Law Working Group, entitled *The Time for Change. The Need for Change. The Case for Change,* recognised that the Child Arrangements Programme was ineffective and called, yet again, for a 'radical reform of the way in which private family law disputes are resolved in and out of the family court'.[38] Work is ongoing to inform young people of their rights and how to access help. The Family Solutions Children's Group recommends in their recently published report that children whose parents separate should be recognised as a discrete target group in need of support and direct services

34 The Observer newspaper, The New Review, Why would you put a ceiling on anyone? 30 April 2023, 10.

35 Ewing, J, 'What About Me? Do we have the 'right' approach to support for children when parents separate?' [2021] *Family Law.*

36 The Rights Idea? Network on Family Regulation and Society (University of Exeter)

37 Coram Foundation, Building Brighter Futures – Empowering children with the skills and aspiration they need to thrive Autumn 2023 Newsletter

38 PLWG Response to Consultation (judiciary.uk) 5.

through the national Family Hubs programmes, and that schools should provide opportunities for young people's forums to discuss family transitions.[39] Some children need specially targeted information and help, such as children with special educational needs and those who are in the process of discovering their gender identity or sexual orientation. The help that can be provided to these young people through mediation is considered further in Chapter 8.

The following chapter explains different stages in children's participation in mediation. The first stage is to explain to parents and carers the opportunity for children to talk with a child professional or family mediator about their views and concerns, while acknowledging parents' reservations about involving their children, and explaining that children report considerable benefits from talking with a person they feel able to trust, and feeling that their views are being heard and respected.

39 Family Solutions Children's Group *What About Me? A Child's Right to Matter* (November 2023).

Chapter 5

Building a professional approach: developing a six-stage process

Stages of the process in outline

The direct involvement of children and young people in mediations with their parents or carers needs to be planned and undertaken in a series of stages. While focusing on each stage, the mediator should also be thinking ahead to the next stage. Details and timescales should be planned carefully to maximise benefits and minimise difficulties. When a talk with the child or children is being agreed and planned, the mediator should pre-arrange a subsequent appointment with the parents, so that their child's messages can be shared with them (assuming that there are messages), as soon as possible after talking with the child. If feedback to the parents is delayed and children have to wait apprehensively for their parents' response, their anxiety may be unreasonably prolonged.

The stages may be listed as follows:

Stage 1 – The mediator explains the process and its objectives to parents/carers and unless there are contra-indications, seeks their consent to the child being offered this opportunity.

Stage 2 – If parents are willing to consider it further, the mediator explains different options for the child's participation and explores these possibilities with the parents.

Stage 3 – Having considered options and reached agreement on the preferred option, the parents explain the opportunity to their children. A personal invitation may then be sent to each child by the mediator, explaining that the child is free to accept or not, but the mediator hopes the child will accept.

Stage 4 – If the child or young person accepts the invitation (as they nearly always do), they should be asked about their preference, such as talking online or meeting in person, with siblings and/or separately. When a date and time have been arranged, the mediator welcomes the child and explains the purpose of the meeting and confidentiality (including the exception for child protection), before encouraging the child to talk freely about their views and wishes and to decide any messages that the child asks the mediator to share with their parents.

Stage 5 – At the child's request, the mediator shares the child's messages and suggestions with their parents/carers together or with each parent separately, or in a family meeting with the child attending as well. The mediator should give children's messages verbally and may show parents their child's written message or picture, but should not provide additional information, interpretations or comments. The mediator should clarify with parents whether they need time to reflect on the message and suggestions before they reach decisions and respond to the child.

Stage 6 – The mediator should offer to have a further talk with the child, as the child may think afterwards of something else they wanted to say, or they may have second thoughts, or the situation may change. If the child wishes to have another talk, their parents' consent should be reconfirmed.

The mediator should maintain a file note throughout these stages, recording progress on a checklist. Copies of these notes and any written messages from children should not be given to parents or provided to third parties. A confidential summary of the outcome of the mediation (but not of the conversation with the child) is sent to parents/carers and they may be asked to share it with their child. If the mediation is ongoing, an interim summary may be provided and the parents may be asked to approve a letter from the mediator to the child to keep the child in the picture.

Stage 1 Explaining the process, recognising concerns and encouraging acceptance

The first stage of explaining child-inclusive mediation to parents and carers needs particular care, because many parents turn it down and it goes no further. As explained in Chapter 3:

> 'All mediators should explain to parents/carers at initial information and assessment meetings, as well as subsequently, that children and young people aged 10 and above should have the opportunity to have a conversation with a professionally qualified mediator or child consultant in which they are invited to give their perspective, in order that parents may take account of those perspectives in any decisions or arrangements that are being made for them.'[1]

This means that mediators who are not ChiM-trained, as well as those who are ChiM-trained and qualified, should provide initial information about this opportunity at information and assessment meetings with each parent/carer separately. Parents may be more receptive to this information on their own, without the stress of their ex-partner's presence or imminent involvement. The opportunity for children to express their views and wishes should be explained in an empathetic conversation, not as a lecture or in a series of tick-boxes. Parents may be inclined to rule out their child's participation because they have concerns about it and do not fully understand its importance and benefits. Concerns that involving their child would cause the child distress or anxiety need to be anticipated before either parent turns down the opportunity for the child to have a say. It is helpful to quote feedback from children and young people who have reported how much it helped them to

1 FMC-Manual-of-Professonal-Standards-Regulatory-Framework-v1.3-Updated-June-2019, Part 6.

talk, and to relate one or two short anecdotes that reassure parents and may amuse them, so that the conversation becomes more relaxed.

Rather than trying to persuade parents/carers to agree to their child being invited, it is helpful to acknowledge common concerns about involving children, noting from eye contact or from their verbal response whether the parents share these concerns. It is important to acknowledge misgivings before either parent declines the offer. Many parents fear that involving children directly will increase their distress, through making them more aware of their parents' disagreements and heightening their conflicts of loyalty. Parents may also fear that the other parent will coach the child on what to say to the mediator, in order to bolster their own position. Mediators need to anticipate these fears and objections at the outset by saying, for example: 'Many parents don't think it's a good idea, because children shouldn't be involved and if the other parent coaches the child on what to say, it would have no value and make things worse.' If one or both parents nod, the mediator might go on to say: 'The idea of your child criticising you is extremely uncomfortable for any of us, as parents. But children are very supportive and they want to help. They say that even when things are OK, talking with the mediator helped them to feel better.' Sometimes, there is a small thing bothering a child or young person which they have not mentioned, because they know their parents have a lot to deal with and do not want to bother them. It may be something that the parents can deal with easily, once they know what it is. It is helpful to give a short example.

The Japanese art of Aikido offers ideas and strategies for mediators. The Aikido practitioner turns around to look in the same direction as their opponent. Facing in the same direction, rather than in the opposite direction, helps to understand the other person's viewpoint so that energy can be used in positive discussion, rather than in promoting a different point of view. Parents need to understand the mediator's role in talking with children, the confidentiality of the conversation and exceptions to confidentiality. Parents also need to understand that children can ask the mediator to share their messages and suggestions with their parents, and that even if their child does not have a message, this does not mean that talking with the child was of no value. Children and young people say they found it very helpful to talk to someone who listened to them. Some said that it made them feel more confident to explain things to their parents themselves, without using the mediator as intermediary. Parents need to know that talking with a mediator helps children to feel better.[2]

Children's self-esteem is increased by knowing that their parents care about their views and that their parents are willing to take their views into account in working out arrangements. This is important information for parents. In the Fortin study with young adults who had experienced their parents' separation in childhood,[3] the researchers enquired about their experience and what had helped them. Many respondents said they had wanted to talk to someone but did not know who would be able to help. Hearing this encourages parents to accept that if they offer their children this opportunity now and they turn it down, their children cannot complain later that they were never asked! Otherwise, how will they feel if their daughter, Kayley, now aged 11, tells them when she is 21 that she had really wanted to talk

2 University of Exeter Wellcome Centre Report and Key Findings, March 2022, see Ch 12.
3 Fortin, J, Scanlan, L and Hunt, J, *Taking a longer view of contact: the perspectives of young adults who experienced parental separation in their youth* (Sussex Law School, University of Sussex) www.sussex.ac.uk/law/research/centreforresponsibilities/takingalongerviewofcontact.

with someone when they separated, but she never had the chance? Parents may ask what the young adults reported from their experience and what helped them. A key message is that 'parents should be more keenly aware of their children's maturity and their capacity to discern their own needs and, unless they are infants, should always consult them before establishing residence and contact arrangements'.[4] A summary of the research findings can be emailed to parents, if they wish.

Resistance on the grounds of additional cost may be reduced if the mediator explains that talking with a child normally takes around half an hour and the charge for this half hour can be split between the parents, that is, a quarter of an hour each. Even when there is more than one child, the mediator's charge should be less than the court application fee and far less than the cost of litigating through lawyers. There should be full public funding for child-inclusive mediation so that it is not restricted to parents who can pay privately. At the time of writing, over 500 accredited mediators on the FMC register provide mediation under the Ministry of Justice's voucher scheme.[5] This scheme entitles parents (and also grandparents) who qualify financially to receive £500 worth of mediation free of charge. Some mediators find it sufficient to cover children's participation, but it may not cover the full cost where further meetings are needed.

Understanding the alternative of applying to the court

Some parents are determined to go to court, believing that a child arrangements order will be more effective than mediation. Parents need to be aware of the timescale for obtaining a child arrangements order, currently almost a year, and should consider whether, if no contact takes place while court proceedings are underway, the likelihood of re-establishing a relationship with the child after such long delay. The court will probably ask a family court adviser or other child expert to provide a report on the child's wishes, feelings and best interests and the judge will take account of this report in reaching a decision. The court makes a charge for a court application and a child arrangements order does not necessarily resolve the difficulties, particularly when parents continue to disagree. On the other hand, when children have the opportunity to talk with a mediator and make suggestions, this eases communication between children and their parents and often results in arrangements that work well in practice. Faced with the court's timescale and envisaging the potential outcome, parents may decide that they have nothing to lose, and possibly much to gain, by taking part in mediation.

Considering contra-indications

Unless there are safeguarding concerns, mediators encourage parents to consider their child being offered the opportunity to talk with a qualified mediator. However, contra-indications should also be considered, such as learning difficulties or mental health issues which might make the child's participation inappropriate.[6] In gathering information from each participant, mediators should enquire whether another professional, such as a psychologist or school counsellor, is working with

4 Ibid.
5 Ministry of Justice spokesman, FMA Conference September 2022.
6 See Ch 8, pp 80–85.

the child or family, to avoid a duplication of roles and responsibilities where the child is concerned. If a social worker is involved, the parents or carers should be asked to agree to the mediator liaising with the social worker, in order to establish whether mediation would be appropriate. The social worker may advise that, if the parents are willing to take part in mediation, this would be helpful alongside the social worker's involvement with the family.

Parents are asked to consent to their child's participation and they also need to confirm their willingness to receive and take account of any messages and suggestions that their child asks the mediator to share with them. If a parent seems unable to recognise their child as an individual with rights, needs and views of their own, and/or if there seems to be a lack of parenting ability to understand and respond to the child's needs and wishes, parents should be signposted to other sources of advice and helping agencies. Inviting a child to come and talk is also unlikely to be suitable if either parent is unwilling to receive and consider the child's messages. Knowing that a parent has no interest in hearing what they think and want is very hurtful for a child, who may experience it as a further rejection.

If Stage 1 is carried out by a mediator who is not ChiM-qualified, parents/carers who take up the offer should be referred to another mediator who is ChiM-qualified, in order to continue the process.

Stage 2 Considering timing and different ways to include children

When is the right time to include children and young people in mediation?

There is no simple answer to this question, because it depends on the circumstances and on the mediator's assessments in designing and structuring the process for the particular family. Parents may be inclined to delay involving their children until a later point in their mediation, not only because they are reluctant to include them, but also because they are understandably preoccupied and overwhelmed by financial worries and uncertainty. If they own a property, they may be unsure whether it can be retained by one parent or whether it will have to be sold. Parents may therefore postpone telling their children what is happening until they are clearer about it themselves. However, children need explanations and reassurance and are well able to understand that major decisions take time. They need to know what is happening in the short term. Mediators should encourage parents and carers to work out interim arrangements for their children, to give them something to hold on to. Interim arrangements can be modified and children's views and suggestions may play an important part in formulating and developing them. Their participation should therefore be considered at an early stage, while major decisions about their residence, schooling and time with each parent can be put on the agenda for continuing mediation with children's further participation. Child-inclusive mediation used to be thought of as a one-off meeting with a child, whereas now it is understood that more than one meeting may be needed.

Talking with children and young people at an early stage enables them to offload their worries and concerns and receive attention they may badly need. There is also the possibility that their views and feelings result in a dramatic change in their parents' plans. In one mediation, there were indications of a significant power imbalance between the parents in which the father held the upper hand. A notional agreement had apparently been reached prior to mediation that the family home would be sold, the net proceeds would be split 50/50 and each parent would purchase a small property with their children, two boys aged 10 and 12, moving between them. The father had moved into rented accommodation pending the sale of the family home and the parents consented to the boys being invited to have a talk with a qualified mediator. This mediator talked with the brothers together and also separately. Both boys were adamant that they wanted their mother to continue as their primary carer. They were strongly opposed to moving to another area and losing their friends and the teachers they liked. The older boy asked if he could speak to the judge. The strength of the boys' wishes was unsettling for their parents, especially for their father, but he came to understand that if the matter went to court, the court could decide that the boys' best interests lay in remaining with their mother in the family home, which should be kept for their benefit, possibly until the younger boy completed full-time education. Each parent took legal advice and agreement was reached on a deferred sale of the family home. The father's relationship with his sons became closer, because he had been receptive to their needs, and they spent more time with him than they had previously been willing to do.

When parents are open to the possibility of their child/children being invited to talk and express their views and feelings, different options should be suggested and discussed. The Family Justice Review recommended that parents should be offered 'a menu of options' in considering ways in which their children may be invited to talk with a mediator or with another child professional, so that their views and suggestions can be taken into account by their parents in making arrangements for their child.

Talking with a school counsellor, therapist, psychologist or other child expert

Some children find it helpful to talk with a counsellor at school, but children often say that they do not like being called out of class, because their classmates tend to tease them. A child may also fear that the counsellor will chat in the staffroom and share information with their teachers. Family matters are regarded as extremely private and children may not tell even their best friends about their parents' separation or divorce. Child counsellors may not meet with both parents, either before or after meeting with the child. They may rely on the child's account of their situation and talk with the child alone. Anecdotal reports from mediators indicate that parents express a strong preference for their child to talk with a mediator, either the mediator they are meeting with themselves, or with a different mediator, rather than with a child expert with whom they have minimal contact.

A different mediator, who is trained in child-inclusive mediation (ChiM)

As previously mentioned, parents/carers may need to be referred to a different mediator from the one who meets with the parents, who may not be ChiM-qualified. The ChiM mediator needs referral details from the first mediator and may meet with the parents before talking with the child. At the child's request, the ChiM mediator conveys the child's messages and suggestions to the first mediator to share with the parents. Alternatively, the ChiM mediator may join a subsequent mediation meeting to give the child's messages to the parents directly.

The same mediator, if ChiM-trained

Using a different mediator from the one who is mediating with the parents avoids combining two different roles while remaining impartial. On the other hand, there can be advantages in using the same mediator throughout, provided the mediator is ChiM-qualified. The mediator who meets with the parents gathers information and impressions from them, as well as providing them with information and explaining options. Many mediators, including members of the Young FMA Forum, report a strong preference among parents for their child to talk with the same mediator, rather than with a different mediator they have not met. Parents want their child to talk to someone whom they themselves know and trust. Children also say that they find it easier to talk with a mediator who knows their family situation and is trusted by both their parents. Mediators who talk with parents and with children gain a fuller understanding of their relationships and concerns and draw from these perceptions in strengthening bridges of communication between them.

Co-mediators

Co-mediators, at least one of whom must be ChiM-qualified, may mediate with the parents and then, with the parents' consent, one or both mediators may talk with their children. Co-mediators who use this model report that it works very well. They find that children are not overwhelmed in talking with two friendly adults and that conversations flow very easily.

Talking with siblings together and/or separately

Children give support to each other and siblings often grow closer together when their parents separate. It is understandable that parents make arrangements for them collectively. However, siblings have different levels of maturity and may have different views and needs. Arrangements that work well for a younger child may not suit an older brother or sister. When siblings express a preference to come together, the mediator may begin by meeting with them together and then offer to talk with each of them separately. A child may not want to talk in the presence of a sibling who thinks differently. However, some ask to continue talking together, because they want to work out a joint plan or different proposals. In one mediation, three brothers in their early teens each wanted a different arrangement. One boy wanted to move between his parents on a weekly 2-2-3 basis, the second wanted alternating weeks and the third wanted to live with his mum and have days out with his dad. The boys decided they would like to be present when the mediator gave their messages to their parents. The parents had not imagined these variations but they agreed to accommodate them. When the family left, they seemed united and much more confident about how they would move forward.

Stage 3 Inviting the child or young person to have a talk with the mediator

Parents and carers should be consulted on the approach they think their child is likely to prefer. The mediator should also discuss with the parents how they will explain the invitation to their child, together or separately, in order to encourage their child's acceptance. With the parents' agreement, the mediator may then contact the child or young person directly. Feedback from many children is that they like receiving an invitation by post, addressed by hand, so that it looks informal. Each child in the family should receive their own letter, worded appropriately for their age, inviting them to have a talk with the mediator either in person, if distance is not an obstacle, or online, if they prefer. The letter can be approved by the parents first, if they wish, and should explain that the child does not have to accept the invitation, but if they accept, the mediator will be very pleased to meet them and hear how things are going for them. The child or young person needs to know that they will not be asked to make choices or decisions and that they can speak freely, without the mediator telling anyone what they say, unless there is need for safeguarding.[7] Mediators may hesitate to mention the safeguarding exception in their invitation letter, but if it is not referred to, there is a risk that a child might report experiencing abuse in a text or email, believing that the mediator will hold this information in confidence. The mediator would then be faced with the dilemma of betraying the child's trust, or condoning the abuse. The exception to confidentiality where safeguarding is needed should therefore be mentioned in the invitation letter, as well as in conversation, and does not appear to cause a problem, as all children receive this information at school. A parent who is abusing a child or colluding with an abuser is unlikely to consent to ChiM.

The invitation letter should explain that the child can ask the mediator to give a message to their parents, if they wish, and that their parents have agreed to listen and consider the message or suggestions. The child's wishes will not necessarily be followed and it is important not to encourage unrealistic hopes ('I wish they would get back together again') or to make a child feel responsible for decisions. An example of an invitation letter is given in Appendix D.

Children may be invited to reply to the invitation by phone or text or via a parent, saying whether they would like to have a talk and if so, when and how would suit them best. Their preference is likely to vary according to their age. Younger children may like to meet the mediator in person, while teenagers often prefer to talk online in their bedroom. Teenagers are glad not to be driven to and from a meeting by a parent who might ask probing questions, or to sit in the car in uncomfortable silence. Young people who prefer to talk online generally have the necessary technical skills and talking online may be entirely natural to them. But there are understandable concerns that if a child or young person talks with the mediator online, they might not be alone. Could another person be present or be listening to the conversation? Older teenagers can usually be relied on to know that they are talking in privacy, with nobody outside the door or even knowing that the conversation is taking place. With a younger child, however, there could be signs that the child may not be alone. It may be more difficult to be sure that the child is alone and the mediator needs to be alert to signs that someone else is present. To check that nobody else is in the room, the mediator may ask the child to move the camera around to show their room and their favourite things.

Adolescents who prefer to meet with the mediator in person may be able to come on their own, without needing a parent to bring them. Older siblings may come alone on different days, but siblings often like to come together and talk as a group, before being offered some individual time and space. Siblings sometimes carry on

7 See Ch 2 on safeguarding.

their parents' arguments with each other, causing further divisions and disputes. An example of a mediation with two siblings who were on opposing sides, physically and emotionally, is included in the following chapter on engaging and talking with children in mediation.

Beginning, and possibly ending, with a short family meeting

When parents are relatively co-operative and there is no risk of a confrontation in front of the children, it may be helpful to begin with a family meeting to introduce the children and the mediator to each other and to help the children feel comfortable before talking on their own. During the introductory meeting, mediators can use various ways to lighten the atmosphere and put children at ease. The parents then withdraw and one or both parents wait to take the children home. After talking with the mediator, some children want to give their messages to their parents themselves, or they may want to be present while the mediator gives their message. The impact on parents is very powerful when they hear from their children directly. If the messages are positive and both parents opt to wait during the mediator's meeting with their children, it may be helpful for all concerned to end with a short family meeting. However, some messages from a child may be difficult for one or both parents to hear and parents may become emotional. It is therefore generally advisable to pre-arrange a separate 'feedback session' with the parents, as soon as possible after talking with the child, rather than keeping the child waiting in another room in a state of tension and anxiety.

Stages 4–6 of the ChiM process are explained in the following chapters, with examples drawn from practice.

Chapter 6

Engaging and talking with children in mediation

Talking with children and young people in mediation means having conversations with them, not plying them with questions and extracting answers for the benefit of adults who 'want to know'. First of all, mediators need to welcome and engage with the child or young person, introducing themselves and explaining in clear and age-appropriate language what mediation means and how it works. The child needs to understand that talking with the mediator requires their consent, as well as both parents' consent, that it is confidential (with exceptions) and that the mediator does not take sides, give advice or decide anything. This initial welcome, with explanation and reassurance, helps children to speak freely, without feeling under pressure and fearing consequences. If the child decides that they would like the mediator to share a message from them with their parents, the mediator undertakes to share their message in the child's own words, without adding their own views or opinion. The parents are encouraged to consider their child's message and suggestions and take them into account in their decisions. Feedback from children and their parents shows that mediators' conversations with children and young people free up channels of communication, so that family members listen to each other and talk together with greater ease and understanding.[1]

Stage 4 Engaging with a child or young person and initiating a conversation

It is not easy for a child or young person to talk to an unknown adult about private family matters. Children need to get to know this person before they can feel safe and trust them enough to talk about their feelings and concerns. Young people, particularly those whose ethnicity differs from the mediator's ethnicity, need to feel the mediator's friendly interest and genuine wish to understand their position and feelings. The child's school may have a high level of ethnic diversity, but in some parts of the country the child may feel isolated and experience racism. There may also be a problem unrelated to the family situation that is causing distress to the child. Mediators need to be careful not to assume that a child's difficulties are invariably family-related.

If the child seems nervous or reticent, the mediator may comment that few people are keen to talk to someone they don't know well. It may be helpful to quote what some other children of their age have said and ask if they agree, or whether they

1 See Ch 12 for feedback from children and parents.

see it differently. A humorous anecdote from a conversation with another child can make them laugh and help them to relax. As previously recognised, warmth and empathy are needed to engage with children and acknowledge their feelings, as well as professional knowledge and skills. If the meeting is in person, the setting should be welcoming and reassuring and there should be paper and coloured pens for drawing pictures and a variety of things to fiddle or play with while the child or young person talks. Provided that this has been checked with parents beforehand, offering soft drinks and biscuits is usually very popular and helps to create a tea-party atmosphere.

The mediator should welcome the child in an easy and friendly way, introducing themselves by their first name and thanking the child for coming. After an initial chat, the child might be asked whether they had heard of mediation before their parents told them they were seeing a mediator. Many schools have peer mediator schemes, but some children say they had never heard of mediation and are not sure what it is. The mediator explains how mediators help parents and children who are going through separation, divorce or other major changes in their lives. Children need to know that they have the right to be consulted about arrangements, if they wish, and that both their parents are willing to consider their views and suggestions. The mediator may mention conversations they have had with other young people, as this helps the child to feel they are not alone. A ten-year-old boy said he was the only one in his class whose parents did not live together. He felt different from the others. He was amazed to hear that around 3.6 million children in Britain live in separated families.[2] He was shown some books and given information about websites that he could access safely, if he wished. Young people who say they like reading can be shown books about separation and divorce for their age-group that they may find helpful, and stories by authors such as Anne Fine and Jacqueline Wilson.[3] A ten-year-old girl said that reading *The Suitcase Kid* by Jacqueline Wilson had made her feel better, because she thought her own family situation was easier than it was for the girl in the story, who complained: 'there were all these arguments about who would get custody of me. I thought they were talking about custard at first. I hate custard.'[4] Or Claudia in '*Step by wicked step*', who tells the other step children: 'Sometimes he phoned to get to talk to me, and from the freezing way Mum went silent the moment she heard his voice, and held the phone away from her as if it were a bad smell, I'd know it was him.'[5]

Mediators need to reassure children that they will not be asked questions to which they must give answers and that they can speak freely, without worrying that they will cause trouble and upset their parents. The aim is to help them feel listened to and feel able to express their feelings, views and wishes with an assurance of confidentiality, except where there is an indication of harm or abuse and safeguarding may be needed. This exception must be made clear at the start of the conversation, after being mentioned in the mediator's invitation letter.[6] Children express great relief when they know they can talk freely, without the mediator reporting everything they say to their parents. 'Daisy' said: 'I liked it because I could tell her what I felt about the whole thing, and … I knew that whatever I said to

2 www.gov.uk/government/statistics/separated-families-statistics-april-2014-to-march-2021-experimental/.
3 See Appendix F for a list of books for children and young people of different ages.
4 Wilson, J, *The Suitcase Kid* (Corgi books, 1992) 8.
5 Fine, A, *Step by wicked step* (Puffin Books, 1996) 33.
6 See ch 5, Stage 3.

her, she would only say the part to my mum and dad that I wanted her to say.'[7] Children understand the major difference between talking privately with a family mediator and being seen by a child professional who makes a report to the court that will be made available to their parents and the judge. If children fear being blamed and held responsible for the court's decision, remaining silent may be the safest option when they are interviewed for a report. In a court case concerning three children, they were intensely loyal to both parents and anxious to avoid upsetting either of them, so all three refused to express any preference.[8]

As in any situation involving a meeting between relative strangers, there are different ways to build trust and make connections. Children need to know that they can ask the mediator to share their messages and wishes with their parents and that their parents have agreed to listen and take account of their messages, without questioning or reproaching their child afterwards about what they said, or didn't say. As previously mentioned in Chapter 2, members of the Family Justice Young People's Board were consulted by the ChiM trainers' group about their recommendations and one member said: 'I especially like the emphasis on parents or guardians not being able to ask children what was discussed or tell them to say anything because I think that's very important'.

Helping the conversation to flow

Children talk more readily when they know the mediator has the trust of both parents. They like to hear that their parents have talked about them. 'Your parents say you like playing football/using the computer/doing art at school.' If the mediator happens to share the same interest, this establishes a connection right away. A girl who said she liked reading was asked about her favourite authors and this led to a conversation in which she and the mediator agreed that they both preferred Philip Pullman's trilogy, *His Dark Materials*, to J.K. Rowling's *Harry Potter* books. A helpful way to engage with a young person is to ask about their favourite hobbies or activities. However, it is important not to delay having a serious conversation with a child or young person who needs to talk and offload their concerns.

It may be helpful to ask whether things have got any better since their parents separated, or whether they have got harder. It is also helpful to enquire about other members of the family, or about friends whose parents have separated, before asking the child or young person about their own feelings. 'How do you think your parents are coping? Are you worried about either of them?' 'Do you have any friends whose parents don't live together? How are they getting on?' 'Do you tell anyone when you are feeling upset or angry, or do you keep it to yourself?' 'Can you talk to a teacher at school, or would you not trust a teacher or school counsellor to hold what you say in confidence?' Rachel, aged 13, who was consulted in a pre-course assignment, said the mediator should be careful not to launch straight into hard questions such as 'What do you want to happen now that your parents have split up?' Rachel thought the mediator should act 'as if you were feeling your way through the tributaries and gradually you would get to the river and the sea where the big questions are to be answered. If you begin in the open sea, the teenager

---

7 Family Solutions Group *'What About Me?' Reframing Support for Families Following Parental Separation*, 12 November 2020, para 87.

8 *B v B (Minors) (Interviews and Listing Arrangements)* [1994] 2 FLR 489.

wouldn't talk at all.'[9] Rachel advised taking things slowly and building up trust with easier questions, such as 'Do you look forward to coming home from school?'

When the mediator is aware of conflict between the parents over contact or shared care arrangements, it may help to put the child at ease by saying something on these lines: 'Children who feel caught in the middle between their parents do their best to keep both their parents happy. I'm meeting with both your parents, so I'm in the middle too. I don't have power to change things, just as you don't, but I'm helping your parents to agree what they think would work better. You may have some good ideas.' The child needs to understand that the mediator is not acting on the child's behalf, or taking their side against either parent, but is seeking to help the family as a whole. Children need conversations, not interrogations. Having conversations with them is a two-way process in language that needs to be easily understood, free from jargon and age-appropriate. They need opportunities to talk about their feelings and concerns and often make suggestions that their parents consider and accept with relief as a workable solution. The mediator may be the only professional, possibly the only person, who is in direct contact with both parents. Encouraging children to put forward ideas and suggestions is more helpful than trying to find 'the truth'.

Different reasons for resisting contact

Children may resist or refuse contact with a parent for many reasons, including abuse by this parent and/or the resident parent's concerns. The resident parent is often accused by the rejected parent of causing 'parental alienation'.[10] When a child or young person is resisting contact, the mediator may mention conversations they have had with other young people who had different reasons for not wanting contact. Some did not like the arrangements, some complained about a parent's behaviour, and some had experienced verbal or physical abuse. Mentioning these different reasons may help to reassure the young person that the mediator is able to respect their reasons, including rejection of a parent or fears of abuse, without being shocked or making judgements. If it should emerge that the child, or another child they know, is in need of safeguarding, the mediator's responsibility to contact the child protection service has been explained previously. A referral for safeguarding enquiries needs to be made with great care, in case reporting the concern would put the child at greater risk.

Many children have a strong sense of loyalty towards a parent whom they see as hurt and betrayed. How does the child think the hurt parent would react if they say they would like to see the other parent? Are they afraid of causing more trouble? Some children want a change in arrangements so that they can have more time for their own activities and friends. Others explain that they do not get on well with the parent's new partner or their children. Children and young people need opportunities to explain their reasons to someone they are able to trust, so that they can feel that their reasons are heard and respected. If children are open to considering possible options and putting forward suggestions, the mediator may ask if they have ideas that they would like their parents to consider. If the young person has not had contact for a long time and possibly never had a

9 Quoted in Parkinson, L, *Adults should talk to kids more* [2012] *Family Law* 350.
10 See Ch 2 on safeguarding and Ch 7 on 'parental alienation'.

close relationship with the parent they are reluctant to see, the mediator could ask whether there is somewhere, such as a sporting event/air show/shopping centre that they would like to go to, if the parent would take them. Or maybe they could just meet for a coffee and see how it goes?

Sometimes, the mediator may sense that a young person is holding back something that they are afraid of sharing. They may say there is something that is worrying them, but they can't say more about it. The mediator could ask how afraid they are of telling someone about it, on a scale of 1–10. If they rate their fear high on this scale, it needs to be acknowledged, first of all, what a heavy burden this is putting on them. A criminal offence may be involved. If the child assures you that they themselves are not being hurt or harmed in any way, perhaps they are supporting someone else who could be very upset or get punished. The child needs to trust the mediator that they will not repeat anything without their permission – with the normal safety exceptions. It is very important to be aware of the high levels of child sexual abuse and children's fears of disclosing it and getting into trouble, or reporting it to someone who might dismiss it as imaginary.[11]

Children's messages to their parents often include practical suggestions, for example, on the frequency and length of overnight stays. Parents have not always imagined what it is like to pack up bags of clothes and school things every few days and lug these bags between two homes and school. A boy aged 12, who was moving every week between his parents, asked to do his homework at his father's home on a Wednesday, instead of going straight to his mother, because there was such a long hill to walk up, and he needed a little rest first. His parents laughed and agreed. When parents and children listen to each other in working out agreed arrangements, their emotional bonds grow stronger, whereas if parents are not interested in hearing their children's views and suggestions, the emotional bonds weaken and may wither away. Parents may accept suggestions from their children that they would not accept from each other. Mediators may use their screen or flip-chart to brainstorm ideas or sketch a calendar to discuss a possible schedule. The following mediation involved highly acrimonious parents and their two children who were split between their parents. Each child aligned with the parent they lived with and continued their parents' fight with each other.

Kelly aged 13 and Fergus aged 11

When their parents separated, 11-year-old Fergus chose to remain with his father in the family home, because his father was a football coach and he and his dad were very keen on football. Kelly, aged 13, chose to leave the family home with her mother. She and Fergus had different interests and little in common. They argued with each other, taking the side of the parent they lived with, so the family was split in half. The parents were in long-running dispute over shared care and contact arrangements. They had agreed that the children should spend alternate weekends with each parent, but this was not working because Kelly was refusing to go to her father, who was now intending to start court proceedings. He accused the mother of encouraging Kelly's resistance. The mother denied this, saying Kelly was staying out late in the evenings and she was having difficulty managing her. The father said Kelly needed discipline. He could see, however, that taking a hard line would only

11 See Safeguarding in ch 2.

drive her further away from him. Both parents acknowledged that they felt stuck, and they consented to the mediator inviting Kelly and Fergus to come and talk, initially together and then separately. The parents warned the mediator that the children did not get on well and were likely to argue. The mediator welcomed Kelly and Fergus together, introduced himself and said he would be glad to talk with each of them separately, as their needs and wishes were likely to differ. Kelly replied that she did not want to talk on her own. She seemed content to sit in silence while Fergus spoke. She fiddled with her long hair which she pulled over her face with a bored expression. When the mediator asked her a question, she repeated 'Whatever' in an offhand manner and would say no more. Fergus explained that he and Kelly did not get on well because they were different, and he found Kelly boring. Kelly sighed. Fergus said he did not want to stay with his mother every other weekend, because he missed playing with his team in football matches. He thought every third weekend would be enough and he would like his mother to take him to football. He offered to go to his mother's for tea every second week, as this would help to bridge the three week gap between his weekends with her. Fergus said he thought it was unfair that Kelly had to miss an overnight stay with her friend, because their parents had swapped weekends at the last minute. The mediator drew a calendar on the flip-chart and wrote up Fergus's preferred schedule, using his chosen colour. Kelly had looked surprised and pleased when Fergus expressed understanding of her position and she began to talk about what she wanted for herself. She said she would be willing to spend every third weekend with her father, provided he would let her go to a party and sometimes stay overnight with a friend. Their suggestions were written up in different colours, sketching out a three-weekly schedule in which each of them would spend a weekend with each parent on their own and have some limited time together. Their proposals were shared with their parents at the next mediation meeting. The parents were taken aback and disappointed that their children's proposals would mean seeing their non-resident child less frequently. On the other hand, they wanted to bring their endless arguments to an end. Having talked it through, they accepted their children's plan and agreed to try it out. Kelly and Fergus were very pleased that their plan was accepted and relationships in the family improved. Kelly became more amenable and the new arrangements worked better. The children felt they had been heard and family relationships became more relaxed.

Checking and confirming the child's message

The mediator needs to keep an eye on the time, allowing enough time to draw things together and bring the meeting to a close. The young person should be encouraged to write down their message or suggestions and check that this is what they want the mediator to share with their parents. If the mediator writes the message, it should be in the child's own words. Mediators should not try to influence the message or rephrase it, but if a child says 'I don't want', or 'I don't like it when', the child can be asked to imagine how they think their parents will react, when the mediator gives them this message. The mediator should repeat what the child has said, to show they have listened, and may then ask the child if they can think of a different way to say it that their parents might hear more easily. Children seem to take this on board readily and may rephrase their message: 'I think it would work better if ...', or 'It would really help if ...' Kathryn Lamb's amusing book, *Is Anyone's Family as Mad as Mine? A Survival Guide for Teenagers,*[12] uses everyday

12 Piccadilly Press, 2006.

vignettes showing that in order to get the kind of response you want, you need to consider how to express your message. Parents enjoy this book too and many of them say they wish they had read it when they were younger.

Before ending a conversation with children, the mediator should tell them that they are welcome to have another talk, if they would like to talk further. A child may think of something else they want to say, or they might change their mind about something. If they would like another talk, they should ask one of their parents if this can be arranged. Some examples of mediations in which a child or young person wanted to talk further with the mediator are given in Chapter 8.

Young people – including children as young as six – sometimes show higher levels of awareness, insight and understanding than those shown by parents, who are often absorbed in their own troubles. Young people nearly always say how much better they feel after talking with someone who listens and respects them and whom they feel able to trust. Talking with children and young people whose parents or carers are taking part in mediation re-connects wires of communication between family members that may have become twisted or broken. Reconnecting wires does not necessarily provide solutions. Some situations cannot be changed. Children benefit nonetheless from talking with a mediator they feel able to trust, who is not writing a report about them or seeking 'the truth'. Tom, aged 14, an only child, showed great insight and understanding in talking about the breakdown of his parents' marriage and continuing difficulties. When the mediator commented that he seemed very mature for his age, Tom said, smiling: 'You should see me when I'm with my mates.'

Anna aged 11 and James aged 7[13]

Anna and James' parents expressed doubts that Anna would want to talk on her own, as she was very shy, whereas James was very chatty. Anna was resisting regular weekends with her father and neither parent wanted to force her. The invitation to the children was discussed and agreed with both parents. Their mother undertook to reassure them that they would not be pressed to say anything, but if they wanted to explain something to their parents, the mediator would help them to do so. The parents agreed to wait in the reception area and if asked to do so, they would rejoin the meeting and listen to what their children said, without getting angry or upset with them. Anna and James accepted the invitation and said they wanted to talk to the mediator together. Anna looked shy and rather nervous, so the mediator started with a question to James.

Mediator: James, do you have friends at school whose parents don't live together?

James: Yes, I do. I have a friend called Gary and his parents have split up.

Mediator: How do you think Gary is getting on – is it OK for him?

James: Well, Gary says the thing to do is to tell your parents jokes to stop them arguing. I tried that ... I tried to tell my Mum and Dad a joke about a monkey but

13 This example was given in Parkinson, L, *Family Mediation* (1st edn, Sweet & Maxwell, 1997) and subsequent editions.

they didn't listen. They went on arguing. Anyway, I hadn't finished making up the joke.

Mediator: You were really trying to help your parents. I think they'd like to know the way you were trying to help. Could you tell them about it?

James: Yes, I will.

Mediator: Sometimes there are small things children don't like that they don't want to bother their parents about them. But small things can hurt a lot.

James: Yes, that's right. Sometimes when I fall off my bike I have a scratch that really hurts and other times I've got a real gash I hadn't noticed.

Anna: What I don't like is when Dad picks me up from school he is talking all the time on his phone and I've told him I don't like it and my friends tease me about it. But he still does it.

Mediator: So you'd like your father to listen and take more notice of what you say?

Anna: Yes, he doesn't listen.

Mediator: What kind of things do you like doing when you go to your Dad?

Anna: Well, I quite like playing on his computer but the thing is, when I tell him I've got stuck, he just comes and takes over.

Mediator: You mean, you'd like him to show you what to do to get unstuck?

Anna: Yes, he just does it all himself.

Mediator: I think he would show you, if he understands you'd like him to show you.

James: Yes, and I want him to show me too.

The children showed insight and sensitivity to their parents' difficulties and made suggestions, increasingly with a strong sense of humour. They were keen to share their ideas with their parents, who looked very apprehensive when they rejoined the meeting but listened attentively to what the children explained. Their eyes filled with tears when James told them he had tried to tell jokes to stop them arguing. But they also smiled. The atmosphere lightened, when both parents understood that they had not 'failed' as parents and that their children were not judging or blaming them. The meeting helped them realise the great importance of listening carefully to what their children said. Things the parents had not noticed, or which they had dismissed as unimportant, were extremely important from the children's perspective. Anna's withdrawal, which had troubled them both, turned out to be her way of showing resentment that when she did tell them something, they usually forgot about it. The parents had not realised the significance of these apparently small things in talking with the children at home, because they were looking for 'something bigger'. Feedback from the children and the parents after the meeting was extremely positive: 'We can talk much more easily now.'

Emily Beausoleil (what a wonderful name for a mediator!) explains the close connections between mind and body and suggests that asking people to stand up and move around is likely to be more effective than using purely verbal methods to reduce tensions.[14] Physical sensations and slight changes in stance, gesture or movement can affect the emotional state of people in conflict. The way we move shapes and even limits how we think, because our perceptions and feelings are grounded in sensorimotor systems. Young people who tend to explode with anger when faced with a situation they cannot handle may be encouraged to dance or sing or take up boxing. Physical movement uses surplus energy and frees the mind from repetitive negative circling.

Leave Me Out of It!

Leave me out of it!
I've had enough.
Stop asking me what I want,
There's no point.

See a mediator? Whatever for?
There's nothing wrong with me!
Who do they think they are?
I'll go, to show willing
But I won't say much.
They won't listen to me
And they'll twist my words.

Well, I'm surprised!
She actually listened,
And we talked a lot.
I feel clearer in my head now,
I think I can talk to Mum
And she won't get upset,
And I can explain to Dad,
And he won't get angry.

The wires that snapped between us
Have re-connected.
They can carry good messages.
After all, we're still a family.

14 Beausoleil, E, 'Dance and Neuroscience – Implications for Conflict Transformation' in LeBaron, McLeod and Acland (eds), *The Choreography of Resolution – Conflict, Movement and Neuroscience* (American Bar Association, 2013).

Chapter 7

Children's messages for their parents

Stage 5 Sharing children's messages with their parents

The messages which children and young people ask the mediator to share with their parents range from simple and straightforward to complex and problematic. One of the simplest and most heart-warming messages was from a young boy who said: 'Tell my parents I know they are doing their best.' This message was very encouraging for his parents to hear, and they continued to 'do their best.' Another boy wanted to know whether he could take his dog with him when he stayed with his father. His dog was his main companion. His father said his dog would be welcome and his mother had no objection to their son taking the dog with him, so the boy and his dog moved together between the two homes and kept each other company. Greatly loved pets are very important to children. 'You trust them and they trust you.'[1]

Sometimes, a child's message takes parents by surprise, because it was not what they were expecting to hear. Parents tend to look through the wrong end of the telescope, seeking to resolve major questions in the long term, whereas children are concerned with the immediacy of everyday life. Parents may be mistaken about the nature of their children's concerns. A recently separated couple asked the mediator to talk with their two sons, aged 10 and 12, because they thought the boys were upset by their separation. When the boys talked with the mediator, they said: 'Oh no, it's not them splitting up that we're bothered about – that's not the problem – it's the swimming!' They explained that their mother was a swimming coach who took them swimming twice a week and urged them to take part in competitions. The boys wanted to play football instead of swimming, but they were anxious not to upset their mother by telling her this. They asked the mediator to give her their message, as they felt unable to tell her themselves. Their parents were very moved to hear their message and the mother cried. They agreed that the father would take the boys to football the following weekend.[2]

Children often explain something to the mediator that is troubling them, saying that they have not mentioned it to their parents because they did not want to bother them. It may be something their parents can easily deal with, once they understand what it is. Katie, aged 14, said she did not like staying at her father's flat because there was no lock on the bathroom door and she was afraid her younger brother or

1 Quote from a child in mediation.
2 With thanks to Cathy Frances, mediator.

her father would come in when she was using the bathroom. The mediator asked her whether it was difficult to explain to her father that she needed a lock on the door? Well, he was always busy and she didn't like to bother him. Katie's message, which she asked the mediator to convey, was to ask her father if he could put a lock on the bathroom door. Her mother knew the reason for Katie's reluctance to stay overnight, but her father thought the mother was keeping their daughter away from him. After hearing Katie's worry, he put a lock on the bathroom door and Katie resumed her overnight stays.

A child's reasons for refusing contact or overnight stays with the non-resident parent may be an obstacle that represents a major problem for the child, but it may be a relatively minor matter for the parents, once they understand it. However, there are also situations in which the child's resistance is more profound and far more difficult to resolve. When it persists, the parent seeking contact is liable to accuse the other parent of causing 'parental alienation'.

'Parental alienation'

'Parental alienation' is commonly understood to mean a child's rejection of one parent, caused by the deliberate or unconscious influence and actions of the other parent. The term 'parental alienation' was coined in the 1980s by a child psychiatrist in the United States, Dr Richard Gardner, who suggested that some children are indoctrinated by their mother to make false allegations against the father. Cafcass defines parental alienation as occurring 'when a child's resistance/hostility towards one parent is not justified and is the result of psychological manipulation by the other parent'. This definition was approved by the Court of Appeal.[3] The court stated in 2017 that 'contact is to be stopped only as a last resort and only once it has become clear that the child will not benefit from continuing the attempt'.[4] Persistent litigation in disputes over contact stokes up embers of bitterness and resentment which continue to smoulder not only between the parents, but also within the child. Family Bridges is a programme for severely alienated children, consisting of an intensive four-day structured programme for the child and their rejected parent, with the aim of rebuilding their relationship.[5] However, only extremely wealthy parents can access this programme and in many cases the child becomes caught in a toxic triangle.

Indications of parental alienation include:

- one parent portraying the other parent in negative terms to the child;
- one parent suggesting that the other parent does not love the child;
- one parent making unfounded allegations or insinuations against the other parent;
- one parent providing unnecessary reassurance to the child about time with the other parent;
- one parent contacting the child excessively when the child is with the other parent.

3 *Re S (Parental Alienation: Cult)* [2020] EWCA Civ 268, [2020] FLR 263.
4 *Re M* [2017] EWCA Civ 2164, [2018] 2 FL 800.
5 Yvonne Parnell, Director, Family Bridges, Lisbon Conference 1 March 2023.

A parent who, for malicious and vengeful reasons, deliberately blocks the child's contact and relationship with the other parent typically does so by denigrating the other parent continuously to the child and/or in the child's hearing, so that the child absorbs and internalises a picture of the other parent as objectionable and possibly threatening, and thus becomes caught in an alliance of implacable hostility. A deliberately alienating parent may fabricate allegations of events that took place when the child was small. The child may absorb and internalise an image of the other parent as unlovable and even dangerous. The child's reports of abuse may be attributed to parental alienation and dismissed. But if implanted memories have been ingrained as 'truth', it may prove impossible to reconcile the child with the rejected parent. An alienated child is the presenting symptom of a damaged or dysfunctional system, and it is essential to consider the individual components of that system, and their interaction, to fully understand why a child why a child rejects, or fears, a good-enough loving parent. There is a risk of unwitting collusion with domestic abuse.[6]

'Parental alienation' and domestic abuse

When contact is withheld by a mother who claims abuse by the father, the father may make counter-allegations of 'parental alienation' in defence.[7] There have been controversial cases involving unregulated 'child experts' who upheld the father's allegation of parental alienation, without listening to the child and taking account of the child's reports of abuse.[8] As the Harm Report pointed out, there is a 'pro-contact culture' which assumes that children benefit from contact, even where a child reports that the parent seeking contact has been abusive.[9] The Harm Report found that 'one consequence of not listening effectively to the child is that the reasons for the child not wanting to have contact with the abuser are not properly understood or taken into account. Listening more carefully to the child may result in a better understanding of whether or not allegations of parental alienation have any merit.'[10] A study at the University of Manchester with 45 women who had alleged domestic abuse by their former partner found that in 39 cases, their former partner (the father of their children) made counter-allegations against the mother of causing 'parental alienation'.[11] In six other cases, the father either threatened allegations of 'parental alienation' or claimed that the mother was mentally unstable. The women reported that the stress they experienced in contested court proceedings over contact caused flashbacks, suicidal thoughts and depression. Some had a miscarriage or an illness such as cancer that they believed was caused or exacerbated by the court proceedings. In 43 of the 45 cases, the court made an order for contact, even where the father had been convicted of child sexual abuse. In one of the other two cases, the court considered that the child was old enough to decide whether to have contact and in the other, the father abducted the child.

6 Shocking impact of family courts on women's health exposed (manchester.ac.uk).
7 Ministry of Justice, *Assessing Risk of Harm to Children and Parents in Private Law Children Cases*, 2020 Final Report.
8 For example, Court of Appeal *Re B (children: policy investigation)* July 2022.
9 Assessing Risk of Harm to Children and Parents in Private Law Children Cases, Final Report, Ministry of Justice, June 2020, 82.
10 See n 5 above.
11 Shocking impact of family courts on women's health exposed (manchester.ac.uk).

Children and young people who withdraw from a parent need to be listened to. If their reasons are not understood and taken into account, lack of knowledge and understanding can lead to unconscious collusion with the alienation process.[12] A pro-contact culture must not take precedence over protecting a child from abuse. The President of the Family Division of the High Court in England and Wales has stated that decisions on whether a parent has alienated a child should be a question of fact – not a diagnosis made by a psychologist.[13] This judgment follows advice from the Association of Clinical Psychologists UK that 'parental alienation', like domestic abuse, is a question of fact – not a syndrome capable of being diagnosed.

Some parents make unfounded allegations of child abuse in angry attempts to denigrate the other parent. When social workers do not find evidence to support the allegations, they may recommend that mediation should take place, or should continue, to help parents rebuild their trust in each other and co-operate better. In one case referred to mediation following prolonged litigation in which each parent had made allegations of child abuse against the other, an investigation failed to find evidence to support the allegations. The parents accepted mediation and, with the mediator's help, reached an outcome in which they withdrew their accusations against each other. They acknowledged that their allegations had been made in anger and through fear of losing their daughters, aged eight and ten. Assisted by a mediator with extensive professional experience in the field of child protection, these parents regained their ability to communicate and co-operate with each other. The parents gave their joint written consent to waive their confidentiality so that their Mediation Summary (Memorandum of Understanding) could be considered by the judge at the court review hearing. The judge approved the arrangements worked out in mediation.

Justified rejection

The Fortin study with young adults whose parents had separated found that 'when children resist contact, they often do so for their own independently formed reasons'.[14] Woodall and Woodall[15] distinguish 'parental alienation' from a young person's 'justified rejection' of a parent, for reasons that the young person can explain and justify. In one mediation, the mother explained that she had grown accustomed to her husband working away from home, until one day she picked up his mobile phone and found text messages indicating that he was in a long-running relationship with another woman. She found the other woman's address and the next time her husband was away, ostensibly for work, she went to this address and her husband opened the door. She divorced him. The father hoped that their two teenage daughters would be willing to maintain their relationship with him, following the divorce. With both parents' consent, the girls spoke with the mediator online and said they despised the way their father had cheated on their mother and that they felt betrayed by him as well. The girls were adamant that they did not want anything further to do with him. By this time, the father had moved to another country where he was living with a different woman. He

12 Whitcombe (n 6) above.
13 *Re C ('Parental Alienation')* (judiciary.uk).
14 Fortin, J, Scanlan, L and Hunt, J, 'Taking a longer view of contact: the perspectives of young adults who experienced parental separation in their youth' [2013] *Family Law* 7.
15 Woodall, K and Woodall, N, *Understanding Parental Alienation* (Charles C. Thomas, 2017).

was disappointed, but not surprised, that his daughters did not want to have any contact with him.

Justified resistance

There are other situations in which a child's withdrawal from a parent may be seen as 'justified resistance', rather than as 'justified rejection'. When a parent leaves home without explanation, children are left adrift in a sea of uncertainty. They are likely to cling to the remaining parent whom they see as their anchor or rock. If they feel abandoned by the parent who has left home – more often, the father – they may express their hurt and anger by rejecting his attempts to contact them. If the mother does not actively support the child's contact with the father, he may give up the struggle. A message, even an apology, from the parent who has left may help the child to relent and accept that their father left their mother, not the child, and that he loves the child as much as ever. When communication has broken down, mediators may need to give a reassuring message from a parent to a child, as well as conveying messages from a child to their parents.

Young children who become caught in conflicts of loyalty may try to be loyal to both parents by telling each parent what they want to hear. A social worker or family court adviser who visits the child in each parent's home may be perplexed by contradictions in their words and behaviour in each setting. If the child feels split between warring parents, their internal security is disorganised and confused. Telling each parent what that parent wants to hear avoids taking one parent's side against the other parent. Contradictory statements from children inflame conflict between the parents, each of whom claims to know 'the truth'. In his novel, *What Maisie Knew*, about a young girl involved in a bitter divorce, Henry James describes her as 'a little porcelain cup in which biting acids could be mixed. She was the little feathered shuttlecock they could fiercely keep flying between them'. Maisie aligns herself with whichever parent she is with, because each parent 'is like an object brought so close to her face that she could not see round its edges'.[16]

Children who reject the parent who has left the family home may be expressing their own hurt. They may also be supporting the remaining parent whom they feel has been abandoned. When a child supports a vulnerable parent in a reversal of the normal roles, the child may not take on this role consciously. Their ambivalent feelings may be too complex to explain in words. Even when children are able to express mixed feelings of pain, anger, and loss, they may fear causing trouble or upset, especially if they fear that what they say will be repeated to their parents and possibly relayed to other people as well. Children and young people need opportunities to explain their reasons to a trustworthy professional who listens to them and respects their views and fears. They may be objecting to arrangements that worked well when they were younger, but which no longer work well for them as they grow up. Teenagers want to spend time with their friends and take part in sport and other activities. 'It's my life too!' They may complain of being treated like a ten-year-old by parents who fail to recognise their need for more space and time with their friends. If young people are able to explain the changes they need, and if their parents are willing to listen and make adjustments, arrangements may

16 James, H, *What Maisie Knew* (Penguin Classics, 1986)18 and 24.

be renegotiated that work well. But without profession intervention, as early as possible, the child's withdrawal may become entrenched.

The following examples are from mediations in which children and young people who were resisting contact with a parent explained their reasons to the mediator.

Difficulties in a child-parent relationship

Both parents said at their separate initial meetings with the mediator that they intended to take property and financial issues to court in divorce proceedings. The mediator asked how their two sons, Kieran aged 11 and Ryan, aged 13, were getting on. Both parents said their older son, Ryan had become withdrawn and increasingly resistant to spending time with his mother. The parents accepted the mediator's offer to talk with the boys, together and separately. Kieran said everything was fine, but Ryan said his mother was often angry with him. He felt that she treated him like his father, because he was rather like his father, and that she loved his brother more than she loved him. Ryan's message to his mother was that he felt she did not love him because he resembled his father, and that he wanted a better relationship with her. His mother broke down in tears when she received his message. She agreed that Ryan resembled his father in many ways and confessed that she tended to 'let fly' at him. She was determined to make amends and sent him a message in response. Relationships improved greatly, not only between Ryan and his mother, but also between the parents, who worked out terms for a settlement on financial and property matters in mediation, without going to court.

In another mediation, the father explained at his initial meeting that the mother had a puppy that was not house-trained. He was about to ask a social worker to call on her to see whether the conditions in her home met basic standards of hygiene. The father said that their children, Julia aged 14 and Giles aged 12, wanted to explain themselves why they were unwilling to visit their mother's home. Both parents agreed to their children being invited to talk to the mediator. Julia said she was disgusted, because she had found 'puppy poo' on the bed in her bedroom. Giles said the whole house stank and he could not play football in the garden, because the grass was full of dog poo. Their mother received their messages with distress and said she felt deeply ashamed. She explained that she had neglected to take her anti-depressants and her situation had got out of control. She was now taking her medication, the puppy was being house-trained and she had cleaned up the house and garden. She offered to send photographs to the children and their father to show the transformation, with further photographs to show that the improvements were being maintained. Julia and Giles cautiously resumed their visits, and their mother told them how deeply she regretted their distress. The puppy became fully house-trained, and Giles enjoyed playing with him.

Difficulties involving a parent's new partner

The parents had separated some months previously and both were living with new partners. Their three sons, aged 15, 13 and 11, were living with their mother and her partner. The boys' contact with their father had broken down and the parents each attended initial meetings and decided to give mediation a try. In mediation, the father accused the mother of not supporting the boys' contact with him. She retaliated by saying he was unreliable and self-centred and that his partner had slapped their middle son and sworn at him. The mediator turned their attention to the boys, asking about their personality, health, education, friends, favourite activities and how they had reacted to the separation. Their mother explained that they did not want to visit their father at his new partner's home, because they felt unwelcome there and got bored, since he could not afford to take them out. He complained of their rudeness towards his partner. The parents were asked how far they had shared the parenting of the boys when they were younger and were encouraged to propose some ground-rules for more harmonious relationships. The parents agreed that the boys should treat their partners with respect. If one of the boys was rude or misbehaved, the partner concerned should ask the parent they lived with to sort out the problem, rather than getting angry and disciplining the boy themselves. The parents arranged to sit down together with the boys and go through the ground-rules with them, inviting their comments and suggestions. The boys asked their father if he would go out cycling with them at weekends, as this would not cost money and they thought it would give his partner a break. They realised that they could be rather noisy. Both partners were consulted and with consensus on the ground-rules, the parents reported that life in both households had become considerably easier.

Children's messages can motivate parents to co-operate

Some separated parents become so embroiled in arguments that they are unaware of the impact of their conflict on their children. Being caught in the middle between warring parents puts a child under great pressure. Children need the fighting to stop. When a mediator shares an emotional message from a child with their parents, they are often shocked by the child's distress. There may be a silence while they absorb the message, followed by willingness to consider possible ways to make things better. In a mediation concerning a nine-year-old girl called Asia, she was moving between her parents every 15 days. Her parents had separated when she was five years old and both were now living with a new partner and had a son, either from their new relationship or from an earlier relationship, before Asia was born. The parents had a very acrimonious divorce and were in long-running conflict over financial matters, child maintenance, Asia's education and upbringing. The father was authoritarian and rigid in his views, whereas the mother tended to fluctuate, but stubbornly resisted his demands. When Asia learnt that her parents were taking part in mediation, she asked to meet the mediator too and her parents gave their consent. Asia told the mediator that she had a lot of anger bottled up inside her and it erupted at school in bad behaviour and fights with her schoolmates. The mediator read a book with her about feeling very angry and managing your anger without hurting yourself or others. The mediator also lent Asia a book about children and divorce to read at home with each of her parents. When they read the book with her, Asia asked if it was her fault that they had split up. Her parents reassured her that it was not. Relationships improved for a time, but in the following summer Asia's father separated from his new partner and her mother had a tempestuous row with her new partner. Asia asked to see the mediator again. The mediator lent her two more books which Asia promised to return shortly. At her third meeting with the mediator, Asia recounted an incident at school where she felt her teacher had blamed her unjustly and punished her. Her parents had gone to the school together to speak up for her and with this joint support from them both, Asia said she was feeling a lot better. She brought a portrait she had drawn of 'my mediator' and asked if she could come again if she needed to.

Conveying a difficult message

Children may find it difficult to tell their parents how they feel. They may ask the mediator to give a message to one parent alone, because the other parent already knows the child's feelings. Children dread causing confrontations between their parents and fear being blamed. Giving children's messages to each parent separately needs to be considered carefully. In cases where a child is confiding in one parent (usually – but not always – the parent they live with), the 'confidante parent' normally agrees to the message being given to the other parent separately. If the child is reluctant to have contact, it would be very hard for one parent to receive a negative message while the other parent sits there with a triumphant, 'told you so' expression. The rejected parent may be angry and defensive or may break down in tears. It would be even more painful for them to show their emotions in front of a gloating ex-partner. Some parents, however, support each other with compassion and may be moved by the distress they see to give each other more support. In these difficult situations, mediators need to tread slowly and sensitively, gauging which approach is likely to be more helpful. Maintaining trust and impartiality are essential. If trust in the mediator is lost as a result of suspicions of bias, the mediation will fail.

Parents' response to their children's messages

The mediator should ask parents how soon they will give their response to their child, so that the child is not kept waiting in a state of anxious uncertainty. According to feedback shared informally between mediators, parents are often deeply moved by their children's messages and respond positively to their suggestions. Court proceedings are often avoided, and where proceedings have been started, they are likely to be discontinued. In a particularly moving mediation, the teenage boy was overcome with relief that his father accepted his wish to live with his mother, once his father had explained to him that for practical reasons it would not work well for him to live with his father.[17]

Children's messages to their parents often include practical suggestions for a change in arrangements that they think would work better for all concerned. Inevitably, there are some disappointing outcomes in which a parent refuses to consider a child's message or rejects the message outright, but these seem to be rare. In one case, the father refused his teenage daughter's request to spend one-to-one time with her when she visited him. The father had remarried and had young children from his new relationship. He said that spending time with his older daughter on her own would mean neglecting his 'new family'. She was deeply disappointed and felt he cared less about her than about his younger children.

When a child or young person is strongly opposed to contact, their refusal may be extremely hard for the rejected parent to accept. However, if an older child explains their reasons to a family court adviser or professional appointed by the court, the judge, having taken account of the adolescent's views and reasons, may decide against making an order with which the young person is unlikely to comply. In a case referred to mediation from the court, the father had started proceedings because his 14-year-old son, Callum, was refusing contact with him. The father was

17 With thanks to Philippa Johnson.

accusing the mother of turning Callum against him and the mother denied that she was doing so. The parents gave consent to Callum being invited to talk with the mediator and he accepted. Callum explained that he had never felt close to his father and related some incidents in which he felt his father had behaved very severely towards him. He said he had grown away from his father and objected strongly to the daily text message his father was sending him, telling him how much his father loved him and wanted to see him. Callum felt his father did not see him as a separate individual with rights of his own, but as a 'possession' that his father could control. Callum resented the pressure from his father and dreaded the court proceedings. He said the stress was affecting his concentration at school and he was falling behind with his schoolwork. His father was very reluctant to accept Callum's request to allow him some emotional space, but after the mediator had talked with Callum on a second occasion, the father sent him a message, saying that although he missed him, he respected Callum's position and would not pursue the court proceedings. Callum received his father's message with huge relief, feeling for the first time that his father was respecting him as a person. There was no further news from the family, but it would not have been surprising to hear that, after a time, Callum made contact with his father on his own initiative.

Children and young people need to understand when they talk with a mediator that their wishes may not be fulfilled, and that the mediator's role is to listen to them and share messages that they would like their parents or carers to consider and take into account. Children need to be clear that the mediator is not acting on their behalf to achieve the outcome the child is looking for. However, even when their dreams cannot be fulfilled, children say that it helped them to talk to a caring person and feel heard and understood. When parents make decisions and arrangements that do not go along with the child's wishes, the mediator should encourage the parents to explain their decisions to their child in a way that will make it easier for the child to accept them.

On Children

Your children are not your children.
They are the sons and daughters of Life's longing for itself.
They come through you, but not from you,
And though they are with you yet they belong not to you.
You may give them your love but not your thoughts,
For they have their own thoughts.
You may house their bodies but not their souls,
For their souls dwell in the house of tomorrow,
which you cannot visit, not even in your dreams.
You may strive to be like them, but seek not to make them like you.
For life goes not backward nor tarries with yesterday.

Kahlil Gibran *'The Prophet'* (1926)

Chapter 8

Shaping the process to fit the child

Each child is unique

When there are several children in a family, it may be convenient to talk about them collectively as 'the children' and make arrangements for them as a group. However, in every mediation where there are dependent children, the mediator should ask parents or carers during initial meetings to describe each child and enquire how the child is getting on. Parents are generally proud of their children and pleased to talk about each of them individually.

Asking questions about each child has several purposes. As well as showing interest and gathering vital information, asking about each child shifts the focus from parents' differences as a separating couple to their shared love for their children and continuing role as parents. In describing each child's personality and interests, parents talk and listen to each other. If one parent is the main carer, asking about the child's stage of development and favourite activities enables the parent with day-to-day care to update the other parent. Parents often describe their child's personality in similar terms, despite disagreeing about arrangements. They may be surprised to find how much they agree. If they are asked to show each other (and the mediator) a photo of their children on their phones, they usually smile at each other's photos. The atmosphere changes and becomes more relaxed. Gathering a picture of each child includes asking how they are getting on at school, their friends and sibling relationships, health, interests and activities, personality and stage of development. Have the parents told their children that they are going to separate or divorce, and have they reassured each child that the separation is not the child's fault? How do the parents know when their child is happy and how do they know when the child is upset? Does the child tell them, or show feelings in behaviour? Almost all parents who come to mediation love their children deeply. Even when they disagree over arrangements, the atmosphere usually lightens when parents describe each child. It is then easier to move on to questions about arrangements. In one mediation, parents who had not been speaking to each other and who were in high conflict over their sons, relaxed visibly as they talked about each boy's personality and activities. The parents then became able to work out time-sharing arrangements. However, there are also situations in which more time is needed for listening and talking. Possible arrangements may need to be worked out gradually, step by step, with opportunities for parents and children to review each step, before they consider and plan the next one.

Stage 6 Arranging further meetings with a child or young person

There are various circumstances in which a single conversation with a child or young person may not be sufficient. Two examples were given in the previous chapter. Asia, aged 9, wanted to speak with the mediator on three occasions, while Callum, aged 14, met twice with the mediator and also spoke on the phone during his summer holidays. Both parents should be asked for their consent to the mediator having further conversations with their child. In these examples, the parents consented readily, because they thought it would ease their child's difficulties. In another mediation, Samantha, aged 12, was very upset that her mother's move to another town 50 miles away had resulted in Samantha changing schools and losing her friends. Samantha blamed her mother and told her father that she wanted to move home and live with him and her stepmother, so that she could continue to go to her old school. When her mother heard this, she told Samantha that if she chose to leave, she would not want to see her any more. Samantha was put in an impossible dilemma. The mediator suggested talking things through again at half-term, a few weeks later. Samantha accepted this offer with relief. When she came the second time, she looked much more cheerful. She said she had settled in her new school and made friends. Rather than moving to live with her father, she thought it would be better to stay with her mother and younger sisters and spend a long weekend at her father's home every other weekend and two weeks in school holidays. Both parents were content with this arrangement and greatly relieved that a further painful disruption in the family was avoided.[1]

Young children may need several meetings with their parents and the mediator, in order to demonstrate to the child that their parents have stopped arguing and can talk together in a calm and friendly way. Otherwise, a young child may be so fearful of another angry scene that the child throws a tantrum to prevent the parents from meeting each other. In one mediation, the mother explained that Sheena, aged three, screamed whenever she saw her father approaching, because she had previously witnessed her parents shouting and hitting each other. The parents were now co-operating and wanted Sheena to have contact with her father, but Sheena was too scared. Her mother explained to her that she could come with her to meet the mediator and there would be toys to play with and her father would join them for a short time and play with her. Sheena said this would be OK. A series of short meetings were arranged in which Sheena and her father played together, while her mother sat quietly and watched them. Sheena regained confidence that it was safe for her parents to meet each other. After these meetings, she was happy to go out with her father, without any distress.

When a child reacts with behavioural problems at home or at school, separated parents tend to blame each other for causing the problem. The more parents argue over who is to blame, the less chance there is of the child receiving help and understanding. Parents who complain that a child's behaviour is attention-seeking may not realise that attention-seeking needs to be understood as attachment-seeking. There can be serious consequences of disrupted attachments, particularly for an infant or young child and especially if the disruption occurs suddenly and

1 This mediation was also referred to in Parkinson, L, *Are You Listening? Conversations with children during parental separation and divorce* December [2021] Family Law 1560-66.

without explanation. Separating parents need to understand the importance of maintaining their child's attachments and prioritising the child's needs and healthy development over their own wishes and claims. Frequent disruptions of routine are harmful for infants and also for children aged four and above if they feel pulled between their parents. Attachment is like elastic. If it is pulled too hard or too often, elasticity weakens and begins to sag. Overstrained elastic may eventually wear out, if adequate support is not provided.

Attachment theory

The formation of attachment is a key process in human development, providing the foundation on which secure relationships are built. Attachment theory was developed in the 1960s by John Bowlby, a child psychiatrist, who defined attachment as a 'lasting psychological connectedness between human beings'.[2] A child's attachment to their parents or carers is a major consideration when arrangements are made for a child following parental separation. Bowlby's studies showed that infants form an emotional and psychological attachment, normally with the mother, from around three months onwards. Maintaining at least one secure attachment to a parent or carer enables the child to feel loved and safe, to develop feelings of self-worth and to be able to trust new relationships.

Ainsworth's 'strange situation' experiments studied infants' reactions to the presence of their mother, their father and two strangers, in varying combinations. The experiments showed four principal patterns of attachment. These were classified as: (1) secure; (2) insecure-ambivalent or resistant; (3) insecure-avoidant; and (4) insecure-disorganised/disoriented.[3] From around six months onwards, a child is able to form an attachment to more than one person. An attachment to both parents increases the child's sense of security and buttresses the child's ability to cope with change.[4] Cohen and Campos[5] found that most infants aged ten months showed attachment to both parents. The incidence of exclusive mother attachment was consistently low, occurring in only about 10% of infants. Lamb[6] found that even at seven months, the age when focused attachments first emerge, infants in the study wanted to be held by, or reached out to, either parent. Cross-cultural researchers suggest that attachment behaviours may be found among infants in different cultures, but the nature of these attachments is likely to be influenced by different patterns of child rearing.[7] As pointed out previously, mediators need to be aware that our concepts of attachment are likely to be viewed from the perspective of our own culture.

---

2 Bowlby J *Attachment and Loss Vol.1 Attachment* (Basic Books, 1969).

3 Ainsworth, M, 'Attachment: Retrospect and Prospect' in C M Parkes and J Stevenson-Hinde (eds), *The Place of Attachment in Human Behaviour* (Basic Books, 1982).

4 Schaffer, H R, *Making Decisions about Children – Psychological Questions and Answers* (Blackwell 1990).

5 Cohen, L and Campos, J, 'Father, mother and stranger as elicitors of attachment behaviour in infants' (1974) 10 *Journal of Developmental Psychology* 146–54.

6 Lamb, M, 'Father-infant and mother-infant interaction in the first year of life' (1977) 48 *Child Development* 167–81.

7 Robinson, L, *Cross-cultural child development for social workers – an introduction* (Palgrave, 2007).

The growth of the child's brain and the harm caused by prolonged stress

Developing an attachment is more than the formation of an emotional and psychological bond. It is a process that changes the architecture of the child's brain. 'The brain, about 30% formed at birth, expands threefold during the first three years and much of the growth of the human brain during this time is experience dependent, meaning that the brain's development is affected by the nature and quality of care the infant receives.'[8] Animal studies have shown that the quality of early care-giving directly affects the brain's growth and development. Similar results have been found in human care-giving.[9] Changes to the brain are made through the stimulation of synapses, such as a parent's smile conveying love to the baby. In the first weeks of life, the number of synapses increases dramatically, depending on the stimulation received. Interactions such as eye contact, tone of voice and caressing stimulate specific parts of the brain and strengthen nerve pathways. If there is a lack of positive interaction, the infant can become insecure or 'anxiously attached'. In her book, *Why Love Matters – how affection shapes a baby's brain*, Gerhardt explains the brain's rapid development in infancy, the importance of secure attachment and the harm caused to an infant's developing brain in experiencing prolonged stress during separation from the primary carer.[10] Infants who are securely attached are able to explore their gradually expanding world, confident of a safe return to their primary carer. As they get older and can understand practical arrangements and lengths of time, children can manage longer periods of separation and transitions between separated parents. Those with multiple attachments have greater emotional resources to draw from. Adolescents' attachments to their parents become looser as they develop greater independence, but they still need the security of knowing that they have a loving family and a stable home. Having a firm base provides roots to tether them as they venture further afield and become independent.

When parents separate, the child's age, stage of development and attachments need careful consideration, so that arrangements can be made that meet the child's needs, rather than the parents' needs.

> 'Attachment in the first year of life, when the brain circuits for attachment are still setting up, is different from attachment in the third or fourth year of life, when the system is going, so to speak. That is, to stress a developmental system while it is organizing in the first year will have a much more negative impact in response to the same stressor than if you did it when the child was four.'[11]

Studies suggest that repeated and prolonged absence from the primary caregiver may be uniquely stressful for an infant or child under four years old. A young child may suffer prolonged stress if separated from their primary carer for periods of time that the child is unable to comprehend. Prolonged stress is particularly harmful for

8 Royal Australian College of Physicians, *Health of children in 'out-of-home' care,* 2006 Sydney: RACP, www.racp.edu.au/download.cfm.
9 Nash, J M, *Fertile minds* (1997) 149(5) *Time* 1.
10 Gerhardt, S, *Why Love Matters – how affection shapes a baby's brain* (Routledge 2004) 31.
11 Schore, A and McIntosh, J, 'Family Law and the neuroscience of attachment', Part 1 [2011] *Family Court Review* 49

children under four years old, because the immature nervous systems of babies and infants are unstable and highly reactive.

> 'Stress in infancy is particularly hazardous, because prolonged stress in the early months of life produces high levels of cortisol that can affect the development of other neurotransmitter systems whose pathways are still being established, making it more difficult for the individual to regulate himself in later life.' [12]

Parents may be shocked to learn that overproduction of cortisol can affect the child's brain permanently. A young father who was recently separated had never looked after his six-month-old child on his own, but he believed he was entitled to have shared care, because 'she's my child too'. He was a caring father, and he was receptive to questions that helped him to imagine how his child would be likely to feel in a strange environment without her mother, who was breast-feeding her. He was shocked to hear about the effects of prolonged stress on a baby's brain and said he wanted to read *Why Love Matters* and work out 'baby friendly' arrangements with his ex-partner in mediation. Leach[13] came under attack from separated fathers for cautioning against overnight stays for children under four years old. Disputes between separated parents over shared care and overnight stays for young children are liable to become gender wars or, as McIntosh called them, 'Baby Wars'.[14] In her keynote address at the inaugural conference of the Association of Family and Conciliation Courts Australian Chapter, McIntosh identified two key conditions that need to be met, so that a young child can be handed over happily between their parents, without becoming agitated:

1 The young child needs to feel safe with, and can be comforted by, either parent.

2 In moving between the parents, the young child does not experience prolonged and potentially harmful levels of stress.

Both these conditions need to be met in making arrangements for young children that support and develop the child's relationship with both parents and ease the child's transfers between them. Rather than seeking each parent's views as to whether a young child should stay overnight with the parent they do not live with, mediators should enquire about the child's stage of development, temperament and attachments, and the current or proposed frequency and duration of overnight stays. Parents, judges and family lawyers, as well as mediators, need to consider the level of stress and disruption of routine that a young child is liable to experience in staying overnight with an unfamiliar carer in an unfamiliar environment. A young child who is handed from one loving parent to the other in an atmosphere of mutual trust and taken to another home not far away, where the child settles easily, has an entirely different experience from a child who is handed to a parent the child knows less well, or hardly at all, in a hostile atmosphere and taken to an unfamiliar place for an unknown length of time.

---

12 See n 8 above, 65.

13 Leach, P, *Family Breakdown* (Unbound, 2014).

14 McIntosh, J, *Beyond the Baby Wars – toward an integrated approach to the post-separation care of very young children*, Keynote address to the inaugural conference of the AFCC Australian Chapter, August 2014.

Loss of attachment

Loss of attachment is a form of bereavement. Bowlby's collected lectures, *The Making and Breaking of Affectional Bonds*,[15] include a chapter on childhood mourning in which he describes three phases of separation and loss as protest, despair and detachment. 'In each of these phases, the child is prone to tantrums and episodes of destructive behaviour, often of a disquietingly violent kind.'[16] Carrie and David Grant adopted a son, Nathan, who had been moved between multiple carers during a short space of time. Nathan was severely traumatised, and his behaviour became increasingly violent. After an incident in which he attacked and injured Carrie, he was removed from the Grants' home by social workers and placed in secure residential care.[17] The impact on a child of severing an attachment that is fundamental to their security is devastating. 'Sometimes roots are pulled out. They get replaced with scars that cut deep, and either nothing can grow, or what does grow is twisted and mixed up.'[18] When a child or young person reacts to their loss with disturbed and acting out behaviour, parents, carers and teachers may need help and support to understand and respond to the child's acute needs. Mental health services for children and young people are critically overloaded and distraught parents or carers need information and support services that can be accessed via their child's school or local Family Hub. If the primary carer becomes unwell, or becomes dependent on alcohol or drugs, there are risks that the child or young person may be taken into foster care or placed in a children's home many miles from the family home. Mediators need to understand and respond to the undertow of loss that some children carry, their emotional and psychological scars and their need to talk with someone they feel able to trust. Loss of attachment and feelings of insecurity are likely to have a particularly powerful impact on a child with special educational needs, such as ADHD or autism.

Children with special needs and disabilities ('SEND')

There has been a great deal of research on conditions such as autism, dyslexia and ADHD in children. More research is needed on neurodiversity in adolescence, when major changes in hormones, the brain and social influences put new pressures on young people. Neurodiversity presents an additional challenge and stressful circumstances may make a young person more vulnerable to mental health issues. About 75% of mental illness begins before the age of 18.[19]

Mediators may be concerned that talking with a child who has special educational needs or disability might cause the child anxiety and distress. However, children with profound learning difficulties have been shown to be capable of expressing views.[20] The UN Committee on the Rights of the Child has stated that children with disabilities should be equipped with, and enabled to use, any mode of communication necessary

15 Bowlby, J, *The Making and Breaking of Affectional Bonds* (Routledge, 1989).
16 See n 8 above, 61.
17 Grant C and D, *A Very Modern Family: Stories and Guidance to Nurture Your Relationships* (Piatkus Publishing, 2023).
18 Stark-McGinnis, S, *Extraordinary Birds* (Bloomsbury, 2019) 86.
19 Blakemore, S-J, *Inventing Ourselves: The Secret Life of the Teenage Brain* (Black Swan, 2018).
20 Lansdown, G, *The evolving capacities of the child* 2005, Innocenti Research Centre, UNICEF/Save the Children, Florence, 4.

to facilitate the expression of their views. For example, when parents have a child who is deaf, the mediator may decide that a conversation with the child would not be possible. However, the local authority may provide a worker for the deaf who uses sign language. In a mediation with a profoundly deaf father and a mother with limited hearing, Bristol City Council provided a helper who acted as a co-mediator in signing for the parents and translating for the mediator. The parents also communicated with the mediator directly, through eye contact and smiling. They agreed contact arrangements for their small son. Rose Ayling-Ellis, an actor profoundly deaf since birth, won the Strictly Come Dancing competition in 2021. Rose campaigns for free classes in Sign Language, a form of communication she describes as 'poetry'. Rose says: 'deaf children should know that nothing is impossible.'

The Barbie doll company has partnered with the UK Down's Syndrome Association to produce its first doll with Down's syndrome. Ellie Goldstein, a British model with Down's syndrome, took part in a campaign to launch the doll, saying 'Diversity is important to me, as people need to see more people like me out there in the world and not be hidden away.' The doll's dress is patterned with blue and yellow butterflies, colours that are associated with Down's syndrome awareness.

Autism

Each child or young person on the autistic spectrum has their own unique set of strengths and challenges. Their abilities are often underestimated. In November 2022, the BBC broadcast an interview in which an eight-year-old girl diagnosed as autistic interviewed a young adult called Holly, who had a similar diagnosis. The eight-year-old was a confident interviewer and she and Holly encouraged each other to be proud of being different. Rather than focusing on deficiencies and disabilities, mediators need to help each child find their own way to express themselves, so that they feel valued and understood. Some children with special educational needs have exceptional abilities and are good at logical thinking and mathematics. Naoki Higashida, a severely autistic Japanese boy, could not communicate verbally, but with remarkable persistence he learnt to use an alphabet grid invented by his mother. Using this grid, he pointed out letters to spell out words which could then be transcribed. Naoki progressed to writing on a computer and when he was 13, he wrote a book to explain things that he did, or could not do, that he wanted other people to understand.

> 'Making eye contact with someone I'm talking to feels a bit creepy, so I tend to avoid it. … Flapping our fingers and hands in front of our faces allows the light to enter our eyes in a pleasant, filtered fashion. Light that reaches us like this feels soft and gentle, like moonlight. But unfiltered direct light sort of 'needles' its way into the eyeballs of people with autism in sharp straight lines. This actually makes our eyes hurt.'[21]

Cathy Frances, a mediator who often meets with children in mediation, has provided an account of her meeting with three children in a family of five children, all of whom were neurodiverse, apart from the middle ten-year-old girl. The two youngest children were severely non-verbal autistic and attended a special school. Cathy writes as follows:

21 Higashida, N, *The Reason I Jump* (English edn, Hodder & Stoughton 2013) 43 and 102.

'The three I saw had obviously talked about what they were going to tell me, because the 10 year old girl said she wanted to spend time being a child when they visited their dad, rather than acting as the parent responsible for looking after the younger ones all the time. "Dad doesn't know how to cope with them." *How did you learn how to cope with them?* "We watched mum and copied her." *How did your mum learn?* "She went on a special training course for autism." *So what do you think your dad should or could do?* "He should do the same course that mum did." In the feedback session, the father agreed that he should take the special training course on autism and that he would do so. The older children also said how excited the younger ones were when they came home from school in a taxi and saw their dad's van outside the house and knew that he was waiting for them. When the father heard this, he agreed he would arrive half an hour early to collect the children, so that the younger ones would know he was waiting and everyone could enjoy their excitement.'

Cathy's meeting with these children was observed by a mediator who had taken ChiM training, but who had not yet met with a child in a ChiM case. This mediator observed that Cathy listened to the children and let them talk, without jumping in with leading questions or providing answers, as the observer mediator thought she might have done herself.

As previously emphasised, children and young people, as well as adults involved in their care, should be consulted about their participation in mediation. When a child has special educational needs, careful consideration should be given to the child's capacity and wish to communicate. Mediators need additional training and skills to adapt to varying levels of capacity. The College of Mediators (COM) collaborated with the Civil Mediation Council (CMC) and a working group including members of Global Mediation, KIDS, Prime Resolution and the Together Trust to produce training and practice standards for mediators to talk with children with special educational needs.[22] Mediators should explore possibilities for the child's active participation and use their antennae to sense and respond to communication difficulties.[23] If a mediator has concerns about talking with a child with special educational needs, or with a parent who does not show enough understanding, the mediator should talk this through with their PPC. A mediator explained to his PPC that he was feeling impatient with a father who showed little empathy towards his son, who had been diagnosed as autistic. The PPC commented that, from the mediator's description, the father sounded as though he might be on the autistic spectrum himself. The mediator exclaimed: 'That's it! That would explain it.' The mediator changed his approach and the relationship between father and son improved.

The National Autistic Society's website provides information on mediation and how to access a mediator.[24] The University of Rochester Medical Centre has also produced helpful guidelines on communicating with a child or young person with autism or Asperger's syndrome.[25] Organisations such as Direct Mediation Services have websites providing helpful information[26] and Action for Asperger's provides

---

22 https://civilmediation.org/wp-content/uploads/2018/12/Professional-Standards-for-Mediators-v1.1-Nov-2018.pdf.
23 www.sense.org.uk/information-and-advice/conditions/autism/#traits.
24 www.autism.org.uk/advice-and-guidance/topics/education/resolving-differences/england/mediation.
25 www.urmc.rochester.edu/encyclopedia/content.aspx?contenttypeid=160&contentid=46.
26 www.directmediationservices.co.uk/autism-and-divorce/.

autism-specialist counselling for those needing help, either on their own account or for others with autism or Asperger's syndrome.[27] Their counsellors have experience of autism or Asperger's syndrome in their personal lives, as well as specialist training.

School exclusion

Data obtained by the BBC Radio's File on 4 programme from 37 local councils in London, the West Midlands, Greater Manchester and Merseyside show that children with special educational needs are five times more likely to be excluded from mainstream schools.[28] In 2022–23, at least 600 vulnerable children were removed from school, either temporarily or permanently, an increase from 512 in 2021–22, in the 31 areas that provided data for both years. Some children are left unsupervised at home and others are sent to pupil referral units, where gangs often recruit them for criminal exploitation. 'Will', aged 13, who has attention deficit hyperactivity disorder (ADHD), was left without a school placement for over a year. A House of Commons select committee found that parents and carers of children with special educational needs often had to 'wade through a treacle of bureaucracy, conflict, missed appointments and despair'.[29] Before applying for an Education, Health and Care Plan or submit an appeal to a SEND Tribunal, an applicant is required to attend a MIAM and file a mediation certificate with their application. Legal aid is available for those qualifying for public funding. Mediators need to adhere to section 20 of the Equality Act 2010.[30]

Mediating with LGBTQ+ parents and children (lesbian, gay, bisexual, or transgender)

> Differences of sex no more wee knew,
> Then our Guardian Angells doe.[31]

Mediators need to be self-aware and sensitive to variations in gender identity and sexual orientation. There has been a steady increase from 2014 onwards in the number of same-sex civil partnerships and same-sex marriages, and adoption figures show one in six adoptions in England by same-sex couples, almost three times higher than a decade ago.[32] Greater awareness of gender identity makes it more possible today for a young person to identify as LGBT (lesbian, gay, bisexual, or transgender). Much depends, however, on those around them accepting the young person's evolving identity.

> 'Can I be myself now, I ask
> my parents in a dream.
> There is a long silence that lasts
> for years, punctuated by half-
> finished sentences.

27 www.actionforaspergers.org/.
28 BBC Radio 4, File on 4, Tuesday 29 August 2023.
29 House of Commons education select committee report into the SEND system, November 2019.
30 www.legislation.gov.uk/ukpga/2010/15/section/20.
31 Dunne, J, *The Relique.*
32 Adoption UK, March 2022.

Yesterday,
As we spoke, my parents
looked at me, and simply said, yes.
Yes, I asked? Yes, they replied,
We love you.' [33]

In another mediation undertaken by Cathy Frances, Cathy met with 'Lauren', aged 13, who had resisted contact with her father for three years because she rejected his racist, sexist and generally extreme views which she had seen on the internet. Her father blamed Lauren's mother, who was now living in a same-sex relationship, for blocking his contact with his daughter. Lauren sent her father an angry letter saying: 'Mum doesn't stop me from having contact, it's my choice not to see you, so stop blaming her!' Lauren told her mother that the mediator was the one person who understood how she felt. This mediation is ongoing.

Carrie and David Grant, in their book referred to above[34] shared their experience of bringing up three biologically female children, now all adults. David Grant was born in Jamaica and brought up in East London by his mother and grandmother, who came to the UK on the Empire Windrush. Carrie was brought up in Enfield by her mother, her father having left when Carrie was seven. Carrie and David's three daughters were all diagnosed on the autistic spectrum and when they reached adulthood, or were close to being adult, all three redefined their gender in different ways and changed their birth names. 'They have all claimed their own piece of ground and their own identity. They really don't want to be like one another.'

Jackie Kay's first novel was about a black jazz trumpeter called Joss Moody.[35] The book starts with Joss's death and the discovery that he was transgender, assigned female at birth and living as a man with his partner, Millie, and their adopted son, Colman, in an outwardly 'normal' family. When Joss dies, Colman is a young adult, and the book describes his shock and feelings of betrayal when he realises that the person he had always known as his father had been designated female at birth. 'Coming to terms' is a phrase that fails to convey Colman's emotional journey to understanding, acceptance and love. Just as Coleman faced difficulties in his emotional journey, when a young person discovers they are non-binary or transgender, their changing identity can pose difficulties for their parents, teachers and other family members. The Grants' book and Jackie Kay's novel are recommended additions to mediators' reading-lists.[36]

St Augustine emphasised the difference between *scientia*, meaning 'knowing about, or being skilled in' and *sapientia*, meaning insight and wisdom. At the fulcrum between the two, St Augustine placed 'the eye of the heart', which he defined as seeing with compassion. Mediators need empathy and compassion and a considerable range of skills in order to engage and talk with children of different ages, different personalities and different family and cultural backgrounds, so that they feel heard at a deeper level. If a mediator experiences difficulty in connecting with an LGBT child, or with a parent who does not accept that their child is LGBT, the mediator should talk this through with their PPC.

33 Chan, M J, *Bright Fear* (Faber, 2023).
34 Grant C and D *A Very Modern Family: Stories and Guidance to Nurture Your Relationships* (Piaktus Publishing, 2023) n 17 above.
35 Jackie Kay *Trumpet* (Picador, 1998).
36 See Appendix G.

Mediators should also be encouraged to read Eris Young's insightful book, *They, Them, Their – a Guide to Nonbinary and Genderqueer Identities*.[37] Parents may have difficulties, but the child's emotional well-being, needs and self-understandings must come first. Young people who are transgender or non-binary may be in particular need of support. Parents and carers need to let go of their own positions and allow themselves to be led by their child's needs and feelings. Although mediation is a short-term intervention, carefully planned support can help to maintain attachments and nurture greater understanding between children, parents and other relatives or key figures. 'Our interwoven lives draw meaning only from each other'.[38]

37 Young E *They, Them, Their – a Guide to Nonbinary and Genderqueer Identities* (Hachette UK, 2019).

38 Rundell, K *Super-Infinite – the Transformations of John Donne* (Faber & Faber, 2022), p 297.

Chapter 9

Mediation with different kinds of families

Family mediation should not be restricted to helping separating birth parents and their children. A family systems approach offers a broader perspective which includes members of extended families and relatives who may have a central role in looking after children and giving them support.

Mediating with extended families and stepfamilies

The introduction of a parent's new partner can be very difficult for children who are grieving the loss of their 'intact' family. If the parent's new partner becomes involved in looking after them, relationships can become strained. The other parent may feel threatened and fear being replaced, while the new partner may regard the children's visits as intrusive. However, a research study referred to in Chapter 11 found that children rarely saw the step-parent as a replacement or substitute for their mother or father and some saw their step-parent as an extra parent or friend.[1] Step-parents and relatives who intervene unhelpfully cause tensions and frictions between 'old' and 'new' families, especially when a step-family includes 'his' children, 'her' children and 'their' children. A father's new partner, who was only a few years older than his daughter, insisted on sitting between father and daughter on the sofa and would not let them have a cuddle. The father was encouraged in mediation to reassure his daughter and his new partner that he loved them both and that they did not need to see each other as rivals.

When both parents are living with new partners, it may be helpful in some circumstances to invite both couples to come to a mediation meeting, preferably with co-mediators. Alternatively, separate meetings with each pair may be more appropriate. Careful assessment is needed to consider the inclusion of other family members and their actual or potential influence, both within and outside the mediation. Mediators need to assess possible benefits and risks in involving them directly. Different ways of structuring meetings need to be explored and pre-conditions agreed, before involving other family members and designing the mediation process. A remarried couple came to mediation with their six children: two were 'his children', two were 'her children' and two were 'their children'. All six children wanted to be included in the mediation. They enjoyed introducing each other to the co-mediators and drew a diagram on the flip-chart to show how they

1 See Ch 11, research on step-families.

all fitted in. They were mutually supportive in helping their parents – birth parents and step-parents – to work out visiting arrangements.

Mediations with grandparents

Many grandparents have an important role in the lives of their grandchildren, as full-time or part-time carers, confidantes, educators and supporters in times of trouble. 'Grandparents are powerful anchors linking children to their memories and identities.'[2] Mothers are more likely to be employed than in previous generations and 25% of employed mothers seek help with childcare from their parents, usually from their mother.[3] Children's bonds with their grandparents are an important source of support that contributes to their well-being.[4] Lucy Frazer, as Parliamentary Under-Secretary of State for Justice, commented in a parliamentary debate in 2018 that:

> 'grandparents play a significant role in family life. There is something special about the bond between a grandparent and grandchild. The loving relationship that is formed often enriches family life. Grandparents provide stability when it is needed. They can give a sense of history and show how important it is to belong to a family. They can give familial support when it is needed.'[5]

Dunn and Deater-Deckard's study found that, during and following separation, many children turned to their grandparents for support.[6] Grandparents were key confidantes for children facing major changes and upset in their lives. Children who felt emotionally close to their maternal grandparents were found to adjust better to their parents' separation and were less likely to be depressed, anxious, aggressive or to have problems at school. They generally felt closer to their maternal grandparents than to their paternal grandparents, whom they knew less well. Another study by scientists at Emory University, Atlanta, Georgia found that a child with an emotionally empathetic grandmother achieved more at school and had fewer emotional problems than children who lacked a grandmother's warmth and understanding.[7]

Grandparents have no automatic right to apply for a child arrangements order. They must first seek the court's permission to apply for an order, whereas in France, the French Civil Code recognises the child's right to maintain personal relationships with grandparents, who can apply to the court directly. There are various circumstances involving grandparents in which mediation can lead to swifter and more positive outcomes than court proceedings are likely to provide. Some grandparents lose

2 Bendall, C and Davey, S, 'The Grandparent 'Problem' – Encouraging a more relational approach to child arrangements via mediation' in Davey and Lindsey (eds), Grandparents and the Law – Rights and Relationships (Hart Publishing, 2023).
3 Gray, A, 'The changing availability of grandparents as carers and its implications for childcare in the UK' (2005) 34(4) Journal of Social Policy 557–577.
4 Hodgson, L-G, 'Adult grandchildren and their grandparents: the enduring bond' (1992) 34(3) International Journal of Ageing and Human Development 209-225; Bendall and Davey (n 2).
5 Lucy Frazer Hansard HC Deb 2 May 2018 vol. 640 182WH.
6 Dunn, J and Deater-Deckard, K, Children's views of their changing families 2001, Joseph Rowntree Research findings 931.
7 Rilling, J et al., The neural correlates of grandmaternal caregiving, Proceedings of the Royal Society B: Biological Sciences, November 2021.

contact with a much-loved grandchild following a breakdown in their relationship with their son or daughter, who is the parent of the child. Some children are looked after by grandparents who need recognition as the child's guardian. There may also be difficulties following the divorce or death of the grandparents' son or daughter, if their daughter- or son-in-law cuts off contact, wishing to leave the past behind. In cases where a parent found guilty of physical or substance abuse has been barred from contact with the child, grandparents may be anxious to maintain their bond with the child, who may be greatly in need of their support. Mediation may also be needed between maternal and paternal grandparents who are sharing the care of a grandchild.[8]

Mediation between grandparents and parents differs not only in being multi-generational, but also in significant power imbalances between grandparents, who have no formal authority, and parents or guardians holding parental responsibility. Awareness of this power imbalance may deter grandparents from considering mediation, because they doubt that the parent will be willing to take part and, if they do, will be unlikely to agree to contact. Grandparents need to be encouraged to try mediation and made aware that the Mediation Voucher Scheme is available to them. Information needs to be disseminated via websites for grandparents and via the grandparents' alliances that have been set up in some areas. An example of a letter to a son/daughter-in-law who is predicted to be unlikely to come to a MIAM is given in Appendix E. An invitation on these lines may be accepted, much to the grandparents' surprise, and may lead to mediation taking place.

Although some grandchildren are too young to express their views and wishes, those who are mature enough to do so should have this opportunity. Mediators should inform grandparents, as well as parents, of the child's right to be consulted if the child is mature enough and wishes to have a say. In France, according to an experienced family mediator, grandchildren are not generally included.[9] In listening to the child or young person, mediators and other professionals need to be aware that a grandparent can be an abuser, rather than a benign carer. Poppy, a young adult who was abused as a young child by her paternal grandfather, spoke out publicly about her abuse in order to 'take away the shame' for survivors like herself and in the hope that in speaking out she would help others and change attitudes.[10] Mediators must always be alert to pick up a child's signal of distress, while appreciating that for many children, a close connection with their grandparents feels 'more than a strand of DNA, it is a rope thrown from the past'.[11]

Mediations concerning adopted, fostered and 'looked after' children

When adoption is arranged in early infancy, infants who feel secure and well cared for can develop strong attachments to their adoptive parents. However, when adoption occurs later, breaking an existing attachment to birth parents, the child is liable to suffer acute loss and their capacity to form new attachments may be

8 Parkinson, L, 'Mediation with grandparents' [2023] Family Law 1002.
9 Scrive, A, 'Médiation familiale et reprise des liens' in Eid and Scrive (eds), Être grand-parent – Entre présence et distance (Chronique social, 2015 Lyon, France).
10 BBC News, 28 July 2023.
11 Enright, A, The Wren, the Wren (Jonathan Cape, 2023)

jeopardised. Even children who were adopted at a very young age and well cared for by their adoptive parents can feel a sense of loss and abandonment as they grow up. Michael Gove MP, who was adopted when he was four months old, explained in an interview that it was only as he got older that he became aware of being:

> 'the cuckoo in the nest ... the sense that you don't have the same genetic make-up as the people who adopted you. If you've had that original early feeling of abandonment, then you worry about throwing all of yourself into something later, because of the fear that if you make a total commitment, you'll face abandonment or rejection again.'[12]

There are various circumstances and ways in which mediators can help adoptive parents, adopted children, birth parents and other relatives to communicate and understand each other better in working out arrangements.

Separating/divorcing adoptive parents and arrangements for adopted children

In mediating between separating adoptive parents, mediators need to be aware of the losses they may have experienced in the past, as well as their difficulties in the present and their needs for the future. Adoptive parents may have tried for a long time to conceive a child of their own and may have tried in vitro fertilisation without success. Although their inability to conceive is no fault of their own, they may feel a sense of failure. The arrival of their own adopted child usually brings great joy, a joy that may be renewed with subsequent adoptions. But if a rift develops in their own relationship, the sense of failure as a couple and as parents may be compounded by feelings of guilt that this is a further major failure. Self-blame and disillusionment may fuel disputes over arrangements for their adopted children. As Lazzarini explains, the sense of failure that adoptive parents often feel is liable to be accentuated by the critical comments of relatives and friends: 'It would have been better if those poor children had been left in their own country'; or 'now that they've separated, they will regret having adopted.'[13]

Adopted children experiencing the separation or divorce of their adoptive parents undergo a second major loss, even if they have no memory of being separated from their birth parents. In experiencing the separation of their adoptive parents, they may become more fragile emotionally and have greater difficulty in forming trusting relationships. After a period of crisis, they may gradually regain stability, but there are risks of a downward spiral. Much depends on the child's resilience in overcoming challenges and on receiving continuing support from at least one person whom they feel able to trust.[14]

Adopted children whose adoptive parents separate should have the opportunity to talk to a trustworthy professional who listens to their feelings, views and wishes. But they often lack this opportunity. In Italy, the participation of the adopted child

12 Gove, M, in The Times Magazine, 24 June 2023, 26–7.
13 Lazzarini, I, The mediator in the face of family complexities, SIMeF national conference, Florence, Italy, October 2013.
14 See Ch 12 on resilience and the example of Bayley, later in this chapter.

was ruled out by the majority of the mediators quoted in Ghezzi's doctoral thesis[15] on the grounds that including children was not part of their training or practice. Only two of the 11 mediators interviewed in the study had met with the children, in one case together with their adoptive parents, and in the other, with the children on their own. Neither of the mediators stated whether the children they spoke to expressed views and wishes that were taken into account by their adoptive parents and which influenced the outcome of the mediation.

Adoptive parents and birth parents in 'open adoptions', regarding birth parents' continuing contact with their children

Open adoption covers any form of contact with birth parents, from face-to-face meetings to occasional letters. Maintaining contact with birth relatives has been found to assist the development of attachments in birth families.[16] However, a report by Adoption UK in 2022 found that support for adopted children and young people wanting contact with their birth relatives is 'not fit for purpose and requires radical improvement'.[17] Only 12% of adopters had been offered any advice or training on establishing or maintaining their adopted child's contact with birth relatives.

Mediators can have a helpful role in facilitating communication between birth parents and adoptive parents and between the child and both sets of parents. It may be difficult, however, to arrange joint meetings between birth and adoptive parents, because, unlike separated couples, they may be strangers to each other. The Post Adoption Centre in London, an independent agency providing counselling and support to adoptive and birth parents and other family members, set up the Contact Mediation Service in the 1990s to assist adoptive and birth parents to negotiate agreements on post-adoption contact. Researchers at the University of Sussex conducted telephone interviews with a sample of the birth and adoptive parents who had used the service.[18] Most of the parents thought their experiences and concerns had been listened to and validated by mediators who had maintained their impartiality. However, birth parents said they had felt highly vulnerable and anxious and many of them had been reluctant to attend a joint meeting with the adoptive parents. Those who did so felt that the authority and control exercised by the adoptive parents created power imbalances that undermined the attempts to mediate. The children in the study, who had an average age of nine, were not offered the opportunity to talk on their own, either with the mediator or with another child professional.

As in any mediation, mediators should begin by arranging separate information and assessment meetings, in person or online, with birth parents and adoptive parents. Where mediation is found suitable and accepted, further separate meetings can be

15 Ghezzi, G, La mediazione familiare nel contesto della famiglia adottiva, doctoral thesis 2006, Università Cattolica, Milan
16 Lowe, N et al., Supporting Adoption, Reframing the Approach 1999, British Association of Adoption and Fostering (BAAF.)
17 Adoption UK Report, June 2022.
18 Kedward, C, Luckock, B and Lawson, H, 'Mediation and post-adoption contact' (1999) 23(3) Adoption and Fostering 16–26.

arranged if preferred, or joint meetings if all participants are willing. There should be opportunities for children and young people to participate and for their views and wishes to be taken into account. With consensus on waiving confidentiality, arrangements worked out in mediation may then be approved by social workers and endorsed by the court, if necessary. There should also be provision for reviewing and modifying arrangements, as children get older.

Adoptive parents and adopted children's contact with their family of origin

Many children who are adopted at an early age enjoy a happy and secure childhood with their adoptive parents, without missing the birth parents they never knew. In adolescence, however, they may feel the need to discover their origins and develop their sense of identity. 'There is an absence, a void, a question mark, at the very beginning of our lives.'[19] A 13-year-old girl, who had been taken into care when she was six years old, explained in a television documentary that she had asked for access to her case files to find out more about her early history. She said: 'I feel a bit lost sometimes.' A boy who had had six placements in three and a half years, said: 'Everyone needs a family.' Tracing birth parents may cause difficulties, because adopted children may not know how to find them, and their adoptive parents may feel threatened by their 'need to know'. DNA testing and global gene banks have opened up new possibilities of discovering birth parents and blood relatives, sometimes, but by no means always, with professional support in initiating contact. Adopted children and young people may also track down a birth parent themselves, through Facebook or other social media, and may contact them in an emotional crisis or in rebellion against their adoptive parents' discipline or views. Mediation services need to be readily available to children and parents caught up in these complex family situations to help them communicate with each other in working out solutions.

The journalist, Kate Adie, who was adopted as a young child, observed from her experience, 'We all need roots. And we need to know about our past so as to be sure who we are.'[20] Kate Adie was adopted when two weeks old by a couple in Carlisle, who returned her to the adoption agency five days later. Her second placement was successful, but Kate acquired a Short Birth Certificate which provided no details of her birth parents, only those of her adoptive parents. Jackie Kay, the writer and former machair (Scottish poet laureate), had a happy childhood and felt greatly loved by her adoptive parents. They supported her when she wanted to make contact with her birth parents. In her memoir, Jackie recounts her awkward meeting with her birth mother when Jackie was 26. 'We don't really know how to converse. There's an uncomfortable intimacy between us.'[21] The book begins with Jackie's unforgettable account of meeting her birth father in Nigeria. First meetings between adopted children and birth parents are fraught with risk. The child or young adult may have created fantasies that are shattered by the reality of the person they meet. If the birth parent shows no interest in them, the result can be a devastating further rejection. For these reasons, guidance should be sought from a specialist adoption worker who can sound out the birth parent's willingness

19 Winterson, J, Why Be Happy When You Could be Normal? (Vintage Books, 2012) 5.
20 Adie, K, Nobody's Child – Who are you when you don't know your past? (Hodder & Stoughton, 2005) 320.
21 Kay, J, Red Dust Road (Picador, 2010).65.

before a meeting is arranged. Jackie Kay realised that the smiling image she had put together of her birth mother did not match the woman who came through the door in the Hilton Hotel in Milton Keynes. 'My birth mother was a sad figure; she'd had a hard life, been in and out of psychiatric hospital, had numerous breakdowns, and survived a son's suicide. I felt a sadness for her life; that somehow, at her expense perhaps, I had got lucky.'[22]

The screenplay for a forthcoming drama called Kin, written by Emma Dennis-Edwards and to be shown on TV, tells the story of Daisy, now 47, who was taken into care when she was ten days old and later adopted by white parents. At the age of 18, Daisy gained access to her case files and discovered that she had been conceived as a result of her mother being raped. The matter had been investigated by police at the time, but not brought to court. Daisy contacted the police and with her mother's consent to testify in court, the rapist was convicted and sentenced to 11 years in jail. Daisy has since led a successful campaign to change the law, so that children conceived through rape are now recognised as secondary victims, making England and Wales among the first countries in the world to confer this status on children born of rape. Mediators who talk with adoptive children who say they want to track down their birth parents need to be aware of these distressing cases, so that they can warn young people of possible disappointments and guard them, if possible, from shattered hopes and illusions.

Adoptive parents and other relatives

Mediators may find that other members of the adoptive family, such as grandparents, can help an adopted child to understand their origins and reasons for their adoption. 'Grandparents are powerful anchors linking children to their memories and identities.'[23] Professors Cigoli and Scabini of the Catholic University of Milan suggest that grandparents – either birth grandparents or the parents of the adoptive parents – can have an important role in supporting the adoption in emotional, psychological and practical ways.[24] The Family Studies and Research University Centre in Milan[25] has carried out research on problems that arise in adoptive families and resources to help them manage and overcome these problems. Many adoption organisations provide excellent post-adoption support. Nonetheless, difficulties may arise from factors such as adoption at a later age, ethnic background, behaviour issues, the presence of other children or strict discipline by adoptive parents. As in the case of Nathan, referred to in the previous chapter, a breakdown in adoption can result in the adopted child being removed from their adoptive parents and placed in a residential home or with foster parents, with varying outcomes.

Adoptive parents and teachers

When an adopted child has learning difficulties, or shows behaviour problems at school, these difficulties can lead to tensions between adoptive parents who want

22 Ibid 67–8.
23 Bendall and Davey (n 2).
24 Cigoli, V and Scabini, E, Family Identity – Ties, Symbols and Transitions (Lawrence Erlbaum, 2006).
25 Family Studies and Research University Centre, When adoptions go through a crisis (Università Cattolica del Sacro Cuore, Milan, October 2019)

more help for their child and teachers who are struggling to control a large class of lively youngsters. There is little reported experience of mediations involving adoptive parents, children and teachers. The Family Hubs called for by the Family Solutions Group could help to build and develop links between adoption agencies, schools – including special schools – and family mediation services.[26]

Two sets of adoptive parents who adopt siblings from the same family.

Mediation may also be needed to help two sets of adoptive parents work out arrangements so that siblings adopted by different parents can have contact with each other. There may be practical difficulties, or a breakdown in relationships between the two families which mediation can help to resolve.

Adoptive parents and social workers, if an adoption breaks down

Adoptive parents are sometimes resistant to their social worker's advice and communication between them may break down. A mediator may help them to explore options, such as providing further support for the adoptive family.[27]

Fostered children

Adoption is intended to be long-term, whereas foster care may be short-term and siblings may be placed separately, losing contact with each other, as well as with their birth parents. A Report from the Children's Commissioner on the Voice of Children and Young People in Foster Care found that most siblings placed with different carers said they wanted more contact with each other.[28]

When children are moved from one foster carer to another, their capacity to form attachments may be eroded. In the second of three documentaries made by Coventry Children's Services for Channel 4,[29] Bayley, aged 17, told the interviewer that she had had seven different foster parents and had stayed in three residential homes. Shortly before leaving her last residential home when she turned 18, Bayley caused major damage to the property and assaulted a staff member. She explained: 'You tend to push people away before they push you away.' Housed on her own in a small flat and expected to fend for herself, Bayley was extremely lonely and vulnerable. She invited all comers into her flat and there was an incident when the police were called. The turning-point came with a change of social worker, who asked Bayley whether there had ever been anyone in her life with whom she had felt able to talk. After thinking about this, Bayley said there had been an art teacher at a school she had once attended, who had crazy hairstyles and wore loads of earrings. She was fun and Bayley had felt able to talk to her. The social worker

26 See Ch 1, n 47.
27 See the Mockingbird programme described below.
28 Children's Commissioner, Report on the Voices of Children and Young People in Foster Care, May 2018, gov.uk, 9.
29 Kids, shown on Channel 4, May 2023.

managed to track down the art teacher, Nina, who said she would be delighted to renew contact with Bayley. With Nina's support, guidance and much hilarity in their conversations, Bayley settled down and began to build the life she wanted for herself. When she was asked: 'How long do you want Nina to remain in your life?' Bayley replied: ''Till she dies.'

The majority of the 100 children and young people who took part in a study on foster care had an extremely positive view of their carers and were grateful for their love and support.[30] But there can be difficulties in adolescence. Lemn Sissay was placed with foster parents as a small baby because his Ethiopian mother, who had come to England to study, was unable to take him back to Ethiopia when she was summoned home to care for her seriously ill father.[31] Lemn's mother was desperate to keep him and refused to sign adoption papers. Lemn was placed in foster care and his name was changed to Norman. The identity of his foster parents was withheld from his mother, so she was unable to find him and take him home. When 'Norman' was 12, his foster parents complained that he was stealing food and that his behaviour was becoming increasingly volatile. They asked the social worker to take him away and 'Norman' was placed in a children's home. Although his foster family was the only family he knew, he never heard from them again. His personal belongings were not sent to him and he had nothing to put in the locker beside his bed in the dormitory. After a year in which he experienced racism and abuse of different kinds, he was moved to another children's home. Lemn's mother's continuing efforts to trace her lost son were blocked. She was repeatedly asked to sign adoption papers and refused. Lemn found solace in music and writing poetry.

Multiple changes of carer leave children with the sense of not being worthy of anyone's love. Mockingbird is an innovative, award-winning programme led by the Fostering Network in the UK to provide sustainable foster care. A 'constellation of support' is arranged for carers and young people to replicate the nurturing relationships and support provided by the extended family. Young people benefit from having a wider network of people who give support and welcome them into their homes and families for an occasional short break.[32]

Ukraine

Many potential foster carers are discouraged by the bureaucracy of the system, whereas the fast-track system used in the Ukrainian Sponsorship scheme, following the Russian invasion of Ukraine in January 2021, led to 100,000 placements for Ukrainians seeking a home in the UK. Mediators in Ukraine are reporting a surge of demand for mediation concerning fostered children who have lost their parents. Tetyana Bilyk, co-founder and former president of the Ukrainian association of family mediators, has set up a working group to develop guidelines for Ukrainian mediators in cases concerning fostered children.

30 Children's Commissioner, Report on the Voices of Children and Young People in Foster Care, May 2018, gov.uk, 13.
31 Sissay, L, My Name is Why (Canongate, 2019).
32 The Mockingbird programme, Fostering Network.

'Looked-after' children

Children who are taken into the care of the local authority may be removed from situations of neglect and abuse, but owing to the lack of properly regulated children's homes, they may be sent hundreds of miles away from their family to live in an unregulated placement commissioned on an ad hoc basis. These children and young people may feel they have been 'taken out of care', or 'left without care'. Some have mental health conditions or learning disabilities and some are on the autistic spectrum. Children and young people with complex needs who reach crisis point need special care, but there is an acute shortage of secure accommodation. After a suicide attempt, 'Becky', aged 12, was put in an emergency placement in a hotel, where she trashed the room and assaulted staff and the police.[33] 'Hurt people hurt people.' Becky was locked in a bare room in a psychiatric hospital for nearly eight weeks. Her only human contact was when meals were put through a hatch in the door. Sir Andrew McFarlane, President of the Family Division, and his predecessor, Sir James Munby, have both expressed outrage at the failure to provide proper care for children in life-threatening crises. In the case of X, Sir James Munby thundered: 'If, when in eleven days' time, she is released from ZX, we, the system, society, the State, are unable to provide X with the supportive and safe placement she so desperately needs, and if in consequence she is enabled to make another attempt on her life, then I can only say, with bleak emphasis, that we will all have blood on our hands.'[34] These high risk situations are unlikely to be referred to mediation, but if help is sought at an early stage, mediators can form part of the holistic, multi-disciplinary support system for parents, carers, children and young people which the Family Solutions Group called for in their report.[35]

In the view of Nazir Afzal, lawyer, prosecutor and author, the justice system prides itself on process, rather than on understanding the experiences of the people with whom it interacts.[36] Mediators, on the other hand, seek to understand people's experience and emotional needs in helping them to consider possible ways forward. To extend their professional training and experience, mediators can gain imaginative insights from the memoirs of writers such as Jackie Kay and Lemn Sissay, referenced above, and fictionalised accounts such as My Name is Leon by Kit De Vaal, Foster by Claire Keegan, Extraordinary Birds by Sandy Stark-McGinnis and Oranges Are Not The Only Fruit by Jeanette Winterson.[37]

Research findings are an essential frame of reference for mediators who talk with children and their parents. Chapter 11 refers to some of the numerous research studies on children's experience of parental separation and divorce.

33 The Observer newspaper, 21 May 2023, 44.
34 In the Matter of X (A Child) (No3) [2017] EWHC 2036 (Fam) s 39.
35 See Ch 1, n 47.
36 Afzal, N, The Prosecutor (Penguin Books, 2023).
37 See Appendix G Some books that mediators may find useful – or just enjoy!

Chapter 10

Mediation between parents and adolescent children

Adolescence is a time of rapid change, with spurts of physical growth accompanied by significant cognitive development and turbulent emotions. Although the brain is almost adult sized by the age of eight or nine, its structure and the way it functions change radically during adolescence. Studies show that the brain continues to develop throughout adolescence into adulthood.[1] An immature brain encourages risk-taking, particularly among boys – smoking, experimenting with drugs, dangerous driving. The opinion of peers is highly influential. Young people are strongly motivated to seek approval from their peers and are hypersensitive to fears of social exclusion. They are susceptible to the influence of social media and vulnerable to online aggression and manipulation. At the same time, young people are caring, sensitive, eager for laughter and fun. Although the heightened neuroplasticity of the brain during adolescence makes young people vulnerable to stress, it also makes them receptive to new learning and creative interventions. In mediating between parents and adolescents, it is important for mediators to have a good understanding of adolescent development, family systems and family dynamics, together with the skills to facilitate intergenerational communication and creative problem-solving.

Erikson provides a framework for conceptualising human development.[2] In the fifth or adolescent stage of his model, Erikson suggests that adolescents are preoccupied with issues of identity, reaching one of two outcomes, either forming a strong and positive sense of self or, defeated by challenges, developing a diffuse or negative identity. Supportive parents build their child's self-confidence and sense of self through their constant love and care and sensitive responses at each stage of development. A study at Lancaster University which explored everyday life and family values among 57 families with teenagers found that respondents described 'family' very positively, as a means of developing love, care, help and trust.[3] Great value was placed, especially by parents, on spending time together as a distinct group. A 14-year-old girl said: 'I am very lucky with my mum and dad ... I can tell them almost anything ... it's because they are very honest with me, I think'.[4] Adolescents want to be treated by their parents as equals, but they also recognise that parents have responsibilities and that having rights brings responsibility. If parents do not notice or care if their teenager stays out all night, or with whom, the

1 Blakemore, S-J, *Inventing Ourselves: the Secret Life of the Teenage Brain* (Black Swan, 2022).
2 Erikson, E, *Childhood and Society* (Norton & Co, 1950).
3 Langford, W et al., *Family understandings: Closeness, authority and independence in families with teenagers* (Family Policy Studies Centre, March 2001).
4 Ibid.

teenager is likely to feel insecure and alone in the world. Boundaries are necessary, and parental boundaries need to be reviewed and negotiated, as children grow up.

Mental health problems or angry rebellion?

Adolescence should provide a space to explore and enjoy life before major exams loom and job-seeking begins. However, an NHS Digital report showed that rates of probable mental disorder among 17–19-year-olds increased from 1 in 10 in 2017 to 1 in 6 in 2021.[5] Periods of lockdown, school closures and social isolation during the Covid-19 pandemic resulted in a sharp rise of mental illness among adolescents. Young people who report low life satisfaction at 14 are significantly more likely to report mental ill health issues at 17, such as self-harming and suicide attempts.[6] About 75% of mental illness begins before the age of 18.[7] The pressure on mental health services is so acute that a quarter of a million children in the UK with mental health problems are unable to access treatment. Only those deemed at highest risk of suicide are likely to be seen.[8]

While an increasing number of adolescents react to stress and social pressure with mental health issues, others react with outbursts of anger and rebellion. Tensions between adolescents and parents are a normal part of growing up. Adolescents want independence and more time with their friends and arguments with parents erupt easily over everyday issues such as household chores, appearance, dating and curfews. Parental boundaries may be flouted openly or in secret. Much depends on how parents react to challenges to their authority. When they handle their teenagers' difficult moods and volatile behaviour more or less successfully, as most parents do, trivial arguments do not threaten the core of the parent-child relationship. Their relationship continues to hold them together, following parental separation or divorce. One study found that children who lived alone with their mother, following their parents' separation, did not differ from those in two-parent families in the warmth and closeness they reported in their relationship with their mother.[9] Over half the children who moved between two households reported positively, especially if they were involved in decisions about how much time they should spend in each household and if their fathers were committed and actively involved in their children's lives. Researchers at the University of Bristol using data from over 5,000 families who took part in the *Children of the 90s* study[10] found that, after taking a range of factors into account, girls whose father was absent during the first five years of the girl's life were more likely to develop depression in adolescence than girls whose father left when the girl was aged five to ten, or than boys in both age groups.[11]

Parents, whether living together or apart, need to back each other up as co-parents and present a caring and united front, so that a recalcitrant teenager cannot play

5 The Lancet Child and Adolescent Health, *Adolescent Well-being in the UK*, September 2021.
6 Blakemore, S-J, *How to help nurture teenage minds, The Guardian*, 11 March 2023.
7 Ibid.
8 According to a report in *The Guardian* newspaper, 16 April 23.
9 Dunn, J and Deater-Deckard, K, *Children's views of their changing families* (Joseph Rowntree Research findings, 2011) 931.
10 See www.bristol.ac.uk/alspac/about/.
11 Culpin, I et al., 'Father absence and depressive symptoms in adolescence' (2013) 43(12) *Journal of Psychological Medicine*.

one parent off against the other. When parents are in conflict with each other, adolescents lose the stability they need to withstand the challenges that threaten to overwhelm them. Parents often blame each other for problems with adolescent children, without seeking to understand how their child is feeling. If parents maintain a rigid position, insisting on discipline without showing enough love and care, they risk losing their relationship with their child. In the most worrying cases, children who feel imprisoned by a controlling parent or carer, with passive acceptance or ineffectual protest from the other parent, may feel driven to run away. In Penelope Lively's story, *The Driftway*,[12] a boy called Paul, whose mother died when he was a small child, has great difficulty accepting his father's new partner, Christine. Paul takes his little sister to a shop to look for a padlock to put on his bedroom door. He tucks the chain in his pocket, 'his mind on the problem of screws, wood and whether there were the right tools at home'. Paul is apprehended for shoplifting, the police are called, and Paul runs away with his little sister, Sandra. She asks 'Where will we go?' Paul does not hesitate. 'We'll go to Gran's.' Adrian Mole aged 13¾, writes in his diary on Tuesday, January 13, 'My father has gone back to work. Thank God! I don't know how my mother sticks him.' A week later, Adrian Mole's mother tells him she is looking for a job. The diary records 'And what will I do during the holidays? I expect I will have to sit in a launderette to keep warm. I rang my grandma up[13] and told her, and she says I could stay at her house in the holidays and go to the Evergreens' meetings in the afternoons. I wish I hadn't rung now.'[14]

Research by the Children's Society[15] shows that running away is often preceded by conflict with parents or carers, family breakdown or poor relationships, experience of abuse or neglect, or problems at school. The police and social services become involved and the young person may be placed in foster-care or in a children's home that may be many miles from the family home. A quarter of the 100,000 children who run away from home or care each year are at risk of harm. There are 'serious shortcomings in a system that is supposed to protect children in care'.[16] Attempting mediation in such situations may seem doomed to failure, yet mediation can be a key to positive change, if parents are willing to listen to their children and respond.

Mediation with Simon, Ruth and their son, Daniel, aged 14

Ruth was seeking a divorce from her husband, Simon, with a child arrangements order enabling her to remain in the family home with Daniel and his sister, Zara. Ruth explained at her initial information and assessment meeting that Simon was opposed to the divorce and unwilling to move out of the family home. She said that Simon was not abusive, but he imposed such extreme rules on the children that she felt her only course of action was to seek divorce, with the children in her sole care. Simon, at his initial meeting, maintained that he was a loving father and that his rules were in the children's best interests. Both parents accepted mediation because, despite being so far apart, each wanted a solution that the other would accept.

12 Lively, P, *The Driftway* (Heinemann, 1972).
13 If you detect a bias towards grandmothers, you are not far wrong!
14 Townsend, S, *The Secret Diary of Adrian Mole aged 13¾* (Methuen, 1982).
15 Children's Society *Here to Listen?* London, 2013.
16 All Party Parliamentary Groups for Looked After Children and Care Leavers and for Runaway and Missing Children, 18 June 2012.

As an example of Simon's rules against which Daniel was fiercely rebelling, Ruth explained that at mealtimes, Simon ordered the children to chew each mouthful a certain number of times before swallowing, and to brush their teeth for a set length of time after each meal. Before the second mediation meeting could take place, there was an explosive row between Daniel and his father which resulted in Simon locking Daniel in his room. Daniel climbed out of the window and, unlikely as this may sound, he turned up at the mediator's office. His mother had told him about the mediation and he did not know where else to seek help. Daniel was extremely upset and scared about what would happen next. He agreed to the mediator contacting his parents to tell them that he was safely with the mediator. Both parents were in a state of shock, having found Daniel missing from his room.

Crisis creates opportunity

Crisis creates opportunity, as well as danger, and Daniel's family recognised that they needed help. Simon, Ruth and Daniel were each seen separately by the mediator for crisis meetings. Daniel said he wanted to live with his mother and sister and that he still loved his father and wanted to see him, but only if his father would treat him with respect and not impose rules he could not accept. Simon received Daniel's messages with remorse and self-blame. He explained that he had suffered prolonged trauma when growing up as a dissident in eastern Europe in wartime, fearing torture and death if he were caught. The shock of Daniel's escape made him realise that his anxiety to protect his children's health and well-being had got out of control. Simon agreed to move out of the family home, at least in the short term, so that Daniel would move back with his mother and sister. The family needed longer term help than mediation could provide, and they were referred for family therapy, where, according to a follow-up contact they made with the mediator, they continued to make good progress.

This dramatic mediation, unpredictable at each stage, has important messages for mediation practice generally. When parents are caught up in anger or depression, they need support themselves, before they can think and act positively and maintain their role as parents. When parents disagree about childcare principles and arrangements for their children, they should be encouraged to consider mediation and gain more understanding of their children's needs, especially during and following separation or divorce. A study at the University of Sussex concluded that the couple relationship is an important focus for early interventions that help parents respond to their children in ways that benefit the child's mental health.[17] Mediation may also be needed between parents and adolescents to resolve issues and improve relationships that are at risk of breaking down.

Mediation between parents and adolescent children

Communication between parents and adolescents is often difficult and liable to break down. Although lack of public funding may be an obstacle, mediators should be ready to mediate between a parent and an adolescent, with the consent of both

17 Harold, G et al., *What Works to Enhance Inter-Parental Relationships and Improve Outcomes for Children* (Early Intervention Foundation, 2016).

parents (or those with parental responsibility) and, of course, with the adolescent's own willingness, even when no mediation is taking place between the parents. One of the challenges in mediating between parents and adolescents is the power imbalance between them. Parents hold authority over their children, whereas although children have rights, they have no power to make decisions on important matters. Adolescents exercise their own kind of power by withholding information from their parents and making themselves unavailable, to the frustration of parents who are trying to speak to them. Can mediators bridge this power imbalance, so that negotiations can take place with joint decision-making and mutually satisfactory outcomes?

Individual information and assessment meetings are essential, as always, to screen for abuse or risk of harm, to understand each person's issues and concerns, to explain mediation and the mediator's role and to build rapport. It is important to acknowledge and respond to parents' needs for understanding and support, before expecting them to give understanding and support to their children. Many parents have not brought up a teenager before and when they are separated/divorced, they tend to blame themselves for having 'failed' their children or, alternatively, accuse the other parent of turning the child against them. It may help them to know that even when parents live happily together as a couple, they can still be at their wits' end with a rebellious teenager whom they discover is taking drugs and/or staying out late at night. Parents need information about the development of the teenage brain and the importance of sleep. Good sleep is particularly crucial when the brain is developing. Several aspects of sleep change during adolescence. Before puberty, melatonin – the sleep hormone – is produced early in the evening. During puberty, there is evidence that the circadian rhythm – the sleep-wake cycle – changes, so that after puberty, there is a delay of about two hours in the sleep cycle of adolescents. As a result, they go to bed late and find it difficult to get up in the morning. Parents worry about their children's excessive use of phones and social media, but concerns that the use of social media is harmful depends on what is being looked at, and whether teenagers are passively scrolling or actively engaging with others.

It is very understandable that tired and stressed parents become exasperated with a lazy and/or rude teenager and more inclined to complain about their child's failings than to praise their achievements. Children need praise. They need to feel valued and to experience success in some field. Receiving praise from their parents builds self-esteem and increases motivation to achieve more. It is useful to ask parents at initial meetings what each child likes doing and what the child is good at. 'Do you tell Alison/Andrew that you are very proud of them? How do they respond to your praise?' Some child therapists recommend parents to keep a 'Well Done!' book and write a positive note in it nearly every day ('thank you for doing the washing-up') and leave it where the young person will see it as they pass by. Another reason for inquiring about children's favourite activities is to encourage parents to relax and enjoy time with their children, such as going out for a walk, watching a football match or playing a game. Researchers have found that some young people express frustration and boredom about time spent with a parent who is inattentive, absent a great deal and lives a long way from their friends. 'Well, my dad was just boring and he never used to do anything with us. We always just used to go round and sit there. … At that age you want to do something, rather than just sit in the house.' (Sabrina, aged 17, reflecting on her experience).[18] Catherine, aged 20, explained

18 Smart, C, 'From children's shoes to children's voices' (2002) 40(3) *Family Court Review*.

how her visits with her father left her feeling devalued: 'He sometimes made you feel that you weren't that important and it didn't matter if you weren't there. He's not warm or emotional, not someone I can talk to about *me*'.[19] Some non-resident parents make too little effort to maintain their relationship with their children. There is great mutual loss when parents give up too readily. Children who feel abandoned need assurances of their parent's continuing love and commitment. Wallerstein and Kelly suggest that 'the visiting parent and child also have a second chance at this critical juncture to break out of past unhappy relations and establish a new bond.'[20] As research studies have shown, the quality of contact is more important from the child's point of view than simply having contact.[21]

Initial information and assessment meetings with parents provide an invaluable opportunity to gather information about each child's personality and interests and relationships in the family, while also giving parents information they need to be aware of, such as changes taking place in their teenager's brain, so that parents do not immediately blame their child for being moody and selfish. Initial meetings with adolescents are similarly invaluable in engaging with them, showing real interest and warmth, and gaining understanding of their perspectives. Young people need to know that although mediators do not provide solutions, they will listen to their concerns and feelings. Carefully managed discussions in mediation reduce conflict and improve family relationships.

Should mediators seek to settle specific issues between a parent and a young person, or focus on transforming the relationship between them?

This important question was raised by Hanna Bobnieva, an Ukrainian family mediator, in an online workshop for Ukrainian mediators on mediating between parents and adolescents. The following example is based on Hanna's account of a mediation with a mother, Maria, and her 12-year-old daughter, Yana.[22]

Hanna's mediation with Maria and Yana

A 35-year-old mother, Maria, applied for mediation at the request of her 12-year-old daughter, Yana, who wanted to improve her relationship with her mother for the sake of her own physical and mental health. The parents and their five children had moved in February 2023 from Ukraine to Germany. They had no relatives in Germany. The relationship between the parents was strained and they lived sometimes apart, sometimes together. The children's ages ranged from 10 months to 8, 10, 12 and 14 years. Maria was not employed, although highly educated. Two individual meetings took place with Maria and Yana, followed by three joint meetings. Maria explained that she was very tired and inclined to shout at Yana

19 Neale, B and Wade, A, *Parent Problems! Children's views on life when parents split up* (Young Voice, 2000) 15.
20 Wallerstein and Kelly *Surviving the Break-Up* (Grant McIntyre, 1980) 131.
21 Fortin, J, Scanlan L and Hunt, J, 'Taking a longer view of contact: the perspectives of young adults who experienced parental separation in their youth' [2013] *Family Law* 104.
22 Quoted with Hanna Bobnieva's consent.

and throw something at her (such as a phone), and abuse her verbally ('You dress like a prostitute'). Maria described Yana as a strong character who protested if she felt injustice towards her or the other children, defending her rights and expressing herself well. Maria said she had problems only with Yana, because the other children were silent and afraid to stand up for themselves. At the preliminary meetings, Yana said it was important for her to have pocket money or permission to work in her free time, to have the make-up and sewing machine that her mother had taken from her, to have a new phone (the previous two having been broken by her mother), and to have her needs respected. Maria was anxious to limit Yana's time on the phone and ensure that Yana did her schoolwork well, helped around the house and treated her mother with respect. Maria had once caught Yana smoking, so she stopped giving her pocket money, even money given by her grandmother. Maria did not give pocket money to the younger children either, in case Yana took it or because the children might buy something harmful for their health. Yana said that if her parents divorced, she would want to live with her father, because her mother insisted on routine and set rules to make sure that the children studied and ate well and looked tidy. Maria was not getting any support from the father, who thought children should be free to grow up and be responsible for their own decisions and actions.

The first joint meeting was very emotional. Maria and Yana were able to hear each other's grievances and pain. Maria apologised for her emotional outbursts, saying she regretted them and that they happened when she was very tired. The second meeting was very constructive and calm, with agreement reached on many issues. Maria and Yana agreed to spend time together, because both felt this was important and necessary for them. Maria supported Yana's desire to cook and buy groceries together. They also agreed on the purchase of a phone and the time Yana would spend on the phone (social networks, films). When Maria asked for help around the house, Yana should help right away. They decided to make a schedule specifying which household duties Yana should undertake and when, so that she could plan in advance.

At the third meeting, Mara and Yana talked about what worked well, what didn't work and how to look for other options. Yana talked about wanting to spend more time with her mother, without the other children. Talking together eased the intense emotions, but issues continued to arise which called for further solutions. 'Since parents and teenagers will continue to live together, should the mediator focus on finding solutions to the issues as they arise, using a problem-oriented approach, or use a transformational approach to improve their relationship?'

In the ensuing discussion, the mediators considered that the first priority was to help Maria and Yana hear each other and resolve immediate issues, as this would increase their motivation to continue with the mediation. The mediator should then address their relationship in order to increase their understanding of each other's needs, build empathy between them and encourage confidence to work out solutions themselves. Hanna's impressive work at both levels was warmly praised. It was suggested that Yana's father should be invited to take part in the mediation and encouraged to give more support to his wife and family. Techniques such as reframing and circular questions can be used to increase participants' understanding of each other's perspectives and feelings. Parents respond to teenage defiance with more empathy when they understand it as a struggle for more independence, while parents' restrictions may be reframed to teenagers as their parent's anxiety to protect them from harm. It may be helpful to ask: 'What do you think is x/y's greatest concern at the moment?' If the dominant concern is not identified correctly, there is an opportunity to clarify and explain. Asking what parents and adolescents enjoy doing together encourages pleasurable joint activities.

Most young people want to help their parents and need opportunities to offer ideas and suggestions that parents often accept with relief. Mediators have a key role in helping families to manage difficult transitions and adjustment to change. Positive outcomes reported by mediators are supported by longer-term research: 'Parents were frequently moved in a lasting way by the feedback they heard from their children. ... The wake-up call to these parents to alter their behaviours around their children and their attitudes about their previous partner was direct, compelling and effective.'[23]

Young people need information about services available to them and encouragement to access help when they need it

When young people have information about the help available to them, they are more likely to access it themselves, instead of reacting to stress with aggressive or violent behaviour or running away from home. Young people are campaigning for better mental health support at schools and colleges and the Office of the Children's Commissioner is supporting this campaign. The RSHE curriculum (Relationships, Sex and Health Education) now includes a mental health well-being module which teaches students how to recognise early signs of mental ill health, how to seek support, and when to speak to someone when they are worried about their own, or someone else's mental well-being. Up to two-thirds of eligible schools and colleges in England can now apply for a grant to access mental health lead training for a member of staff in their school. The target should be 100%. Discussion groups in schools, youth clubs and sports centres encourage openness and sharing among peers. Children and young people also need to be able to talk to a professional who listens with empathy and respect and who, at their request, can help their parents/carers understand and respond to their concerns. The Munro review emphasised that 'treating children and young people as people, not objects, requires spending time with them to ascertain their views, helping them understand what is happening to them and taking their wishes and opinions into account in making decisions about them.'[24] Adults need to be ready to listen, rather than passive or even resistant to a child's participation in decision-making. The report of the Family Solutions Children's Group, 'What About Me? The child's right to matter', published in November 2023, calls for concerted action in all spheres – education, family law, professional services and social care – on hearing and taking account of young people's views and concerns on matters of great importance to us all, from the right to vote in elections to action on climate change.

23 McIntosh, J, Wells, Y and Long, C, 'Child-focused and child-inclusive family law dispute resolution' (2007) 13(1) *Journal of Family Studies*.

24 *The Munro Review of Child Protection – a child-centred system* (Department for Education, 2011).

Chapter 11

Children's experience of parental separation and divorce

Research on children's experience of parental separation and divorce is so extensive that a short overview is bound to be selective and incomplete. However, findings from studies in a number of countries concur to a great extent, providing a strong foundation for mediators' work with separated parents and their children. Above all:

> 'it is critical to recognise that children are at risk of harm when parents separate. Family breakdown is a time of great vulnerability and research has consistently shown that unresolved parental conflict is harmful to children. Destructive inter-parental conflict affects children of all ages, across infancy, childhood, adolescence, and even adulthood. The way in which parents communicate with each other impacts children's long-term mental health and future life chances.'[1]

Children's views of 'family'

The separation of their parents is liable to upset children profoundly because it disrupts their lives and the security of being part of an 'intact' family. A study by Virginia Morrow at the Centre for Family Research at the University of Cambridge gathered the views of 183 children aged from 8 to 14 on what being part of a family meant to them.[2] The study was conducted in two parts of East Anglia, a rural area and a large town with a population of British Muslims originally from Pakistan. From the children's perspectives, being part of a family means having love, care, mutual support and respect. Claudia, aged 12, said: 'It doesn't matter if you're rich or poor, as long as you love each other. Of course, you're going to have arguments and stuff, but if you love each other it doesn't really matter, does it, what sort of family you're in?' Tara, aged 13, defined 'family' as 'a group of people which all care about each other. They can all cry together, laugh together, argue together, and go through all the emotions together. Some live together as well. Families are for helping each other through life'.[3] The children wanted to be able to have a say in arrangements, but not asked to make decisions themselves.

When Dame Rachel de Souza became Children's Commissioner for England, she said her immediate priority was to hear children's views on what was most important to them in the post-pandemic world. Her office launched the Big Ask,

1 Family Solutions Group Report, November 2020.
2 Morrow, V, *Children's Perspectives on Families* (National Children's Bureau and Rowntree Research Findings 1998) 798.
3 Ibid 2.

a collection of questions for children aged 4 to 17 about their lives, fears, hopes and plans. Over half a million children responded to the survey and 80% of respondents said they were happy with their lives and optimistic for the future.[4] However, children's mental health and well-being gives cause for concern. Before the Covid-19 pandemic, 1 in 9 children had a probable mental disorder. By 2020, the rate had risen to 1 in 6. The Children's Commissioner explained: 'They want someone to talk to when they are worried or upset. They want easier access to support when problems are emerging so they don't start to build up.'[5]

Children's experience of separation

Almost half of children in the UK are growing up outside the traditional nuclear family.[6] Some children experience more than one separation, if the parent they live with forms a new relationship which breaks down as well. Some parents separate suddenly, with many issues unresolved. If children lose touch with the parent who leaves home, the longer the break continues, the harder it becomes to rebuild the relationship. A study at the University of Exeter found that about a quarter of children whose parents separated were liable to lose contact within two years with the parent who left home (usually, their father).[7] Wallerstein and Kelly's study with 60 divorced families in California[8] described the distress of children who lost contact with a parent to whom they were closely attached. ChildLine, the national helpline for children, has reported that many children do not know what is happening and do not want to trouble stressed and worried parents with their questions.

> 'Through most of the calls, there was a picture of children … lacking or being refused information or feeling unable to talk with their parents or ask them questions for fear of upsetting them further.'[9] 'We needed to know what was going on, what was happening, how things would work out … We needed help from outside but there just didn't seem to be the right person to turn to. No one seemed to be there to help us, especially us, the children. Mum and Dad had the lawyers but we had no one.'[10]

In a study involving 467 children aged from 5 to 16 who had experienced their parents' separation, 25% said no one had talked to them about the separation when it happened. Only 5% said they had been given full explanations and a chance to ask questions.[11] It was left to the mother in over 70% of families to tell the children about the separation. Some mothers told their children only that

---

4 The Big Ask: Big Answers | Children's Commissioner for England (childrenscommissioner.gov.uk).
5 De Souza, R, *Briefing on Children's Mental Health Services 2020/21*, Foreword.
6 Family Solutions Group Report, November 2023.
7 Cockett, M and Tripp, J, *The Exeter Family Study: family breakdown and its impact on children* (Exeter University Press, 1994); Trinder, L, Beek, M and Connolly, J, *Children's and parents' experience of contact after divorce* (Joseph Rowntree Foundation Research Findings 2002) 092.
8 Wallerstein, J and Kelly, J, *Surviving the Break-Up – how children and parents cope with divorce* (Grant McIntyre, 1980).
9 Childline Report, *Unhappy Parents, Unhappy Children* 1998, 13.
10 Lyon, C, Surrey, E and Timms, J, *Effective Support Services for Children' and young people when parental relationships break down – a child-centred approach* (University of Liverpool, 1998) 5.
11 Dunn and Deater-Deckard, *Children's Views of their Changing Families* (Joseph Rowntree Research Findings, 2001) 931.

their father had left, without any explanation.[12] One girl told a researcher that her mother 'didn't understand how I felt. She was too busy being angry'.[13] A boy said to the researcher: 'You're the first person who's ever bothered to ask me how I felt'.[14] Children worry about their parents more than is generally recognised, particularly if they fear for a parent's safety. They worry if a parent becomes depressed, or resorts to substance abuse, or turns to their child for support.

If children do not receive explanations, reassurance and support, their reactions may include:

1 *Confusion, anxiety and alarm.* If parents do not explain what is happening, young children are confused and alarmed by a parent's sudden disappearance and may fear that the remaining parent will disappear as well.

2 *Strong reconciliation fantasies.* Children may continue to hope that their parents will get back together and make up fantasies to comfort themselves.

3 *Aggression.* A child's anger often stems from feelings of loss and rejection. The sense of loss when one parent disappears from their lives, often unaccountably, may result in aggressive behaviour towards siblings, parents and at school. The remaining parent may be so preoccupied that the child receives less attention, increasing their sense of loss and rejection.

4 *Guilt.* Young children may imagine that they are to blame for their parents' problems. They may assume that their naughtiness was the reason for the parent leaving them.

5 *Regression.* Children may show their anxiety and insecurity by lapses in toilet training, bed-wetting, increased clinging behaviour and feeding problems.

6 *Increased fears*, such as fear of the dark.

In the early stages of separation when parents are under particular stress, they may find it difficult to work out arrangements for their children. A study at the Centre for Research on the Child and Family at the University of East Anglia found that maintaining children's contact with the non-resident parent needed commitment from both parents and encouragement from the resident parent.[15] To maintain children's relationship and contact with the parent who leaves home, help and support may be needed at an early stage of separation, or even before separation takes place. Wallerstein and Kelly found that:

> 'the relationship between visiting father and child is at its most malleable immediately after the father has moved out of the household and as the visiting pattern emerges. The foundations of the new visiting relationship are laid down during the immediate post-separation period. The visiting parent and child also have a second chance at this critical juncture to break out of past unhappy relations and establish a new bond.'[16]

Wallerstein and Kelly's study was criticised for being based on a non-representative sample of divorcing families in California who were offered therapy in return for participating in the research. Nevertheless, the emphasis on the importance

12 Cockett and Tripp (n 6).
13 Mitchell, A, *Children in the Middle* (Tavistock, 1985) 94.
14 Ibid 81.
15 Trinder Beek and Connolly (n 6) 092.
16 Ibid 131.

of early intervention is a key message for mediators and Wallerstein and Kelly's account of children's distress offers unique insights for working with families during separation. Wallerstein also studied the long-term effects of divorce on children, finding that children and young people may continue to react in the longer term to stressful conditions in the post-divorce family. The findings shed light on 'the complexity of interacting family processes, and on the unexpected 'sleeper' effects of childhood experience'.[17]

The Chinese ideogram for 'crisis' combines two characters, one meaning 'danger' and the other 'opportunity'. Individuals are more ready to accept outside intervention in the early stages of crisis. Help 'purposefully focused at a strategic time is more effective than more extensive help given at a period of less emotional accessibility'.[18] As time goes by, the range of options tends to narrow, positions become entrenched and attitudes harden. The study by Fortin, Scanlan and Hunt with over 400 young adults who had experienced their parents' separation during their childhood found that, as adults, 75% of respondents were still in touch with their non-resident parent.[19] There was a strong correlation between a close pre-separation relationship between the child and the non-resident parent and its continuation into adulthood. Non-resident parents who had a good relationship with their children prior to the separation were more likely to maintain it post-separation, despite geographical distance and parenting problems. The study showed that the foundations of successful contact are laid down pre-separation and the child's relationship with each parent is a major factor in their adjustment to parental separation.[20]

A number of studies of children's perspectives following their parents' separation have found that it is the quality of relationships that matters most – the child's relationship with each parent and the parents' relationship with each other.[21] Good relationships in the post-divorce family are more important for children than the quantity of time they spend with each parent. Carol Smart and her colleagues at the University of Leeds carried out a series of in-depth interviews with children over several years to understand their perspectives on post-divorce residence and contact. Maintaining their attachments and having good relationships mattered more to them than days and times agreed by parents[22] Liz Trinder at the University of Exeter emphasises two key messages:

> 'first, is the critical importance of enabling children to have some influence over arrangements. ... The second key research message is that the overwhelming focus on apportioning children's time reflects an adult rather than a child

---

17 Wallerstein, J, 'Long-term effects of divorce on children' (1991) 30(3) *Journal of the American Academy of Child and Adolescent Psychiatry* 359.

18 Rapoport, R, 'The state of crisis – some theoretical considerations' in Parad (ed), *Crisis Intervention* Family (Service Association of America, 1965) 30.

19 Fortin, J, Scanlan, L and Hunt, J, *Taking a longer view of contact: the perspectives of young adults who experienced parental separation in their youth* (Sussex Law School, University of Sussex) www.sussex.ac.uk/law/research/centreforresponsibilities/takingalongerviewofcontact.

20 Hawthorne, Jessop, Pryor and Richards *Supporting children through family change* (Joseph Rowntree Foundation Findings, 2003) 323; Fortin et al, (n 18).

21 Cockett and Tripp (n 6); Lewis, Papacosta and Warin, *Cohabitation, separation and fatherhood* (Joseph Rowntree Foundation Findings, 2002) 552; Trinder et al., *Making contact: How parents and children negotiate and experience contact after divorce* (Joseph Rowntree Foundation Research Findings) 092.

22 Smart, C, 'From Children's Shoes to Children's Voices' (2002) 30(3) *Family Court Review*.

agenda. If it were children who made applications or decided cases or redesigned the family justice system, then it is likely that most would want to refocus the attention of adults on the quality, rather than the quantity of relationships'.[23]

Studies show that parental separation is a process rather than an event, beginning before one parent leaves the home and continuing long afterwards. The way in which parents manage their separation is more critical for children's well-being than the separation itself.

Children's experience of contact arrangements

Smart and Neale studied how divorcing parents negotiated arrangements for their children and the researchers also talked with the children in these families.[24] Fifty-two children in the study ranged in age from 5 to 22, with the majority aged 8 to 15. Some children were co-parented, some lived with one parent and had regular contact with the other parent, while others never, or rarely, saw their non-residential parent. The researchers found that above all, children and young people wanted civility between their parents and if possible, mutual regard or respect. Siblings of different ages may not want the same arrangements. Smart and Neale[25] found that boys in some families were happy with arrangements that did not suit their sisters, while some older siblings were unhappy with arrangements that worked well for the younger ones. The Fortin study made a similar finding that 'different children will be satisfied with different amounts of contact ... the quantity of contact is less important than the quality of the child's experience'.[26] The young adults in this study were asked how far they had been able to express their own views about contact and the extent to which their views were taken into account, what they wished had been done differently, and what impact they felt the contact they had experienced as children was making in their adult lives, particularly on their current relationships with their parents. Had their views about contact had changed as they grew older, including their opinion of its value and how they thought their parents had dealt with it? The findings showed that contact needs to be continuous. The young adults who had unbroken contact throughout their childhood were most likely to rate their contact positively. When contact had broken down or was not maintained regularly, this was generally attributed to the non-resident parent's lack of commitment to the child. The young adults described parents who had neglected their parenting role in the aftermath of the separation and became less emotionally available, leaving their children feeling alone and unsupported. Children often concealed their distress in their efforts to be loyal to their parents. In the Fortin study, young adults said that if they had felt ignored by their non-resident parent or obliged to follow adult pursuits, this had signalled their lack of importance to this parent. Children are more likely to withdraw if they feel unloved or if they blame the non-resident parent for causing the separation. Many respondents said they wished their parents had managed their separation and post-separation parenting more carefully. However, when contact was lost,

23 Trinder, L, 'Shared Residence: a review of recent research evidence' [2010] *Family Law* 1192-97.
24 Smart, C and Neale, B, *Family Fragments?* (Polity Press, 1999).
25 Smart, C and Neale, B, 'It's My Life Too – Children's Perspectives on Post-Divorce Parenting' [2000] *Family Law* 163–69
26 See n 18 above.

very few respondents thought their resident parent had tried to undermine their relationship with the other parent. 'In contrast, a strong and consistent theme in both the telephone survey and the interview data was the extent to which resident parents had encouraged the relationship between their children and non-resident parents.'[27] The researchers concluded that 'when children resist contact, they often do so for their own independently formed reasons.'[28]

Impact on children of prolonged parental conflict

There is clear evidence that prolonged conflict between separated parents is harmful to children and associated with high risks of the child developing mental health issues and other problems.[29] A study at the University of Southampton found that children who experience prolonged conflict between their parents are at risk of a range of negative effects, including emotional and behavioural difficulties, troubled relationships with family members and peers, problems in settling and achieving at school and poorer health.[30] The Fortin study found that parental conflict not only has a psychologically damaging impact on children, but also impairs their relationship with both parents, often well into adulthood.[31] One respondent gave the following advice to separating parents:

> 'Keep in contact with the child and talk to each other a lot about what's going on. Have an agreed plan about what you're going to do with your child for the next week, two weeks to a year, what do you want to happen. Don't involve your child in your arguments, keep them away from it and talk to them about what's happening… keep on telling them that you love them and it's not their fault.'[32]

Children who move between battling parents are profoundly disturbed by their arguments, especially if they are given hostile messages to carry between them. A young child may throw a tantrum in an attempt to prevent their parents meeting and having another argument. 'Everything is all right as long as I don't let Mum and Dad speak to each other'.[33] High levels of conflict between parents have been shown to have poor outcomes for children, including anxiety and depression, academic failure, substance abuse, conduct problems, criminality, peer problems and adversely affected brain development.[34] Children's experience of their parents' separation is more damaging if parents become overwhelmed by their own problems and unable to support their children as they did previously. Some young adults develop severe emotional difficulties and attribute them to having no one to confide in as children.

27 Fortin et al. (n 18) 6.
28 Ibid 10.
29 Family Justice Review, Final Report, November 2011; Harold, G and Sellers, R, 'Inter-parental Conflict and Youth Psychopathology; an Evidence Review and Practice Focused Update' (2018) 59(4) *Journal of Child Psychology and Psychiatry*; 'Harm Report' *Assessing Risk of Harm to Children and Parents in Private Law Children Cases*, Final Report, Ministry of Justice, June 2020; Family Solutions Group Report, *What About Me? Reframing Support for Families following Parental Separation,* 12 November 2020.
30 Reynolds et al. *Parental Conflict: Outcomes and interventions for children and families* (Policy Press and Research Paper, University of Southampton, 2014).
31 See n 18 above.
32 bid110.
33 Six-year-old child quoted by Cockett and Tripp, The Exeter Study 1994, 43.
34 Adam, H, 'Time for Climate Change in the Family Justice System' [2022] *Family Law* 996.

Shared care

Prior to the Children Act 1989, researchers found that a joint custody order encouraged the continuing involvement of both parents and mitigated 'the profound sense of loss characteristic of so many children of divorce'.[35] However, the Norgrove Report rejected a legal presumption in favour of shared parenting after separation, because 'it is interpreted in practice by counting hours spent with each parent, disregarding the quality of the time'.[36] Separated parents who believe they are entitled to equal time with their children count the exact number of hours that their child spends with each parent. They may decide that the child should move between them several times a week, or spend alternate weeks with each parent, without imagining the child's experience in moving constantly from one home to the other. 'We forget things we want – like toys and music stuff. It takes a lot of doing, getting it from the other house.' A 17-year-old girl reflected that: 'It didn't work for me having two bases, because you've got like two bedrooms and two of everything and I was getting mixed up who I was.'[37] When parents share the care of their children on a 50/50 basis, or nearly equally, without considering the children's needs and concerns, children are seen as possessions, rather than as individuals with their own rights and views. An Australian study of children's satisfaction with post-separation arrangements found that children in shared care were less satisfied than children in other kinds of arrangements and were more likely to want to change them. The researchers concluded that 'equal or substantial sharing of time may in some circumstances be an arrangement better suited to parents than to children'.[38] Trinder made a similar finding in her review of research on shared care arrangements that parents are likely to be more satisfied with these arrangements than their children, and fathers more so than mothers.[39]

Steinman[40] found that shared care arrangements can work well for children where:

- there is good co-operation and communication between parents and clarity about who is responsible for which tasks;
- both parents are willing to be flexible, within a clear structure and travelling time is not too long and tiring for the child;
- the child is free from worries about being fair to both parents;
- practicalities are sorted out: having duplicates of some things in each home avoids the child having to carry everything to and fro all the time;
- the child's friendships and activities are respected – this becomes increasingly important as the child gets older;

35 Abarbanel, A, 'Shared parenting after separation and divorce: a study of joint custody' [1979] *American Journal of Orthopsychiatry* 49; Morgenbesser, M and Nehls, N, *Joint Custody: an alternative for divorcing families* (Nelson Hall, 1980).
36 Family Justice Review Final Report 2011, para 4.23.
37 Neale, B and Wade, *A, Parent Problems! Children's views on life when parents split up* (Young Voice, 2000) 12–13.
38 McIntosh, Smyth, Kelaher, Wells and Long *Post-separation parenting arrangements and developmental outcomes for infants and children* (Family Court of Australia, Attorney-General's Department, 2010) 78.
39 see n 22 above.
40 Steinman, 'The Experience of Children in a Joint Custody Arrangement' (1981) 51 *American Journal of Orthopsychiatry* 403–14

- parents listen to their child and are able to hear when the arrangements need adjusting.

The young adults in the Fortin study[41] advised that shared care works well for children only if parents live close to each other, so that children can attend the same school, and parents need to be on good terms with each other and able to provide their children with two sets of rooms, clothes and school equipment. The children themselves need to be happy with the arrangements. Smart[42] identified three criteria that distinguish successful shared care arrangements from unsuccessful ones:

1 whether children's needs are prioritised, or arrangements are based on the needs and wishes of the parents;

2 whether arrangements are flexible rather than rigid;

3 whether children feel equally 'at home' with both parents.

Elizabeth, aged nine: 'Sometimes I get confused on Mondays and after school, if I've just been at my mum's, sometimes I go to my mum's instead of my dad's.'

Harold, aged 11: 'My dad lives round the corner from my mum. We sleep Mondays, Wednesdays, Fridays and Sundays at my mum's and Tuesdays, Thursdays and Saturdays at my dad's.'

Tom, aged 12: 'It's OK for me, because ... we normally go from school to the other house, then it's all right because we can say goodbye in the morning and we'll be able to forget about it in school.'[43]

Multiple transitions and adjustments in stepfamilies

Another significant factor in children's adjustment to parental separation is the degree of physical and emotional upheaval they experience. Murch found that 20% of children whose parents divorced lived with one parent and then moved to live with the other parent.[44] Children who experienced three or more different family structures were likely to describe themselves as 'often unhappy' or 'miserable'. Findings from several studies have shown that five years after their divorce, half the parents who were the main carers of their children had remarried. The children were living with the new step-parent and in many cases also with the step-parent's children.[45] 'In my family I have five parents – my mum and my step-mum, then my dad and my other step-mum, and then my half-sister's dad, and my brothers and sisters and then there's all the pets of course' (Sonya aged 9[46]). When the non-

41 See n 18 above.

42 Smart, C, 'Equal shares: rights for fathers or recognition for children?' [2004] *Critical Social Policy* 484.

43 Three children quoted by Neale and Wade *(n 36)* 9.

44 Murch, M, *Justice and Welfare in Divorce* (Sweet and Maxwell, 1980).

45 Bane, MJ, 'Marital disruption and the lives of children' (1976) 32 *Journal of Social Issues* 103–17; Leete, R and Anthony, S, 'Divorce and Remarriage' (1979) 16 *Population Trends* 5– 11.

46 Quoted by Neale and Wade (n 36) 21.

resident parent has a new partner, the child needs time to get to know and like the new partner.

Research studies show varying relationships between children and step-parents.[47] Dunn and Deater-Deckard undertook a study with 467 children aged from 5 to 16 who had experienced their parents' separation. Around a quarter of the children lived in a stepfamily and most of the stepfamilies included children from both parents' previous relationships.[48] As mentioned in Chapter 9, some children saw their step-parent as an extra parent, while others saw their step-parent as a friend. Parents can be reassured that children rarely see the step-parent as a replacement or substitute for their mother or father. Although they may not feel emotionally close to their step-parent, 91% of the children who were consulted about their views thought that a step-parent should be a parent or a friend, or both. Some children said, however, that they did not like being disciplined by a step-parent and 50% resented taking second place to the step-parent's children, or to children born to their own parent and the step-parent.

Children want to have a voice and be heard

A review by the NSPCC of UK research studies undertaken between 1990 and 2003 found that children had not known where to go for help and had rarely sought professional help. Twenty years later, young people continue to call for information and support. In the course of preparing their report, 'What About Me? The Child's Right to Matter', the Family Solutions Group consulted 112 members of the UK Youth Parliament, aged 11–18. 74% said they had not known who to ask for support during family separation and the majority did not know of any services that could help them.[49] Young people who had seen a professional reported mixed experiences, some saying that the professional had not believed them, had not talked directly to them and had not provided help when asked. Children's most persistent plea is for age-appropriate information to help them understand what is going on and where to seek help. They want someone they can talk to confidentially, whom they trust, who listens to them and who helps them to think through problems without making them feel responsible for decisions.[50]

Studies have found that most children want a say in matters affecting them.[51] Some young people express frustration and even fury at being ignored. A 15-year-old girl said bitterly: 'We are people too and shouldn't be treated like low-lifes just because we are younger. I think kids deserve the same kind of respect that we are expected to give so-called adults'.[52] In the Fortin study, the majority of the young adults said they had wanted an opportunity to talk to someone about their feelings and

47 Ferri E and Smith D *Step-parenting in the 1990s* Family Policy Studies Centre 1996.

48 Dunn J and Deater-Deckard K *Children's views of their changing families* 2001, Joseph Rowntree Research *findings* 931.

49 Family Solutions Group *What About Me? The Child's Right to Matter* November 2023.

50 Gorin S *Understanding what children say: Children's experiences of domestic abuse, parental substance misuse and parental health problems* 2004 Joseph Rowntree Foundation 514.

51 Morrow V Children's Perspectives on Families' 1998, Centre for Family Research, University of Cambridge *Rowntree Research Findings 798;* Fortin J, Scanlan L and Hunt J, Sussex Law School, University of Sussex *Taking a longer view of contact: the perspectives of young adults who experienced parental separation in their youth* January [2013] Fam Law 104.

52 O'Quigley A *Listening to Children's Views* Joseph Rowntree Foundation 2000 p. 30.

needs, but had not had an opportunity to do so.[53] When children were frightened of, or disliked a parent, they were more likely to say that the child should be able to decide who they should live with. These children did not opt for mutual negotiation or participation – they wanted the right to decide. They also did not want to have their views ascertained in a brief and alien intervention in which children receive a sudden invitation to participate, followed by no further professional interest, giving them the impression that they are simply 'negotiation fodder'. Rather than seeking to ascertain a child's wishes and feelings, Smart and Neale recommended that professionals should have conversations with children about family matters. Jake, aged 11, said: 'I think there should be some kind of agreement between the children and the parents as to what should happen. I think the people who are involved should get to decide, not by themselves, but by helping each other to reach some kind of agreement as to what would be best.'[54] Mark, aged 15, said: 'He should get a say in it, he shouldn't just be left out, I mean, it's his life as well.'[55]

Children and young people need to be informed of their right to have a say and encouraged to talk about their views and concerns. In a video shown at the annual conference of the Family Mediators Association in September 2020, members of the FJYPB said:

> 'We want more information on how our views can be better represented in mediation processes following parental separation. We want our wish to be heard recognised as our right to be heard under UNCRC 1989, Art 12 (1).' [56]

The role of mediation in encouraging cooperation and agreement

Mediation is easily bypassed or rejected by parents who believe that the court will resolve matters to their satisfaction. The applicant may be determined to go to court and the respondent is not required to attend an Information and Assessment Meeting (MIAM) to consider mediation. Both parents, not only the applicant, should be required to attend an information and assessment meeting and they should be provided with a written hand-out quoting parents' experience of mediation and outcomes in the longer term, compared with their experience and outcomes in court proceedings. A two-year study of court proceedings over children showed that 'hammering out a deal and getting contact going does not in itself repair relationships or address the underlying or embedded conflict that probably gave rise to the contact dispute in the first place.'[57] 'Parents find the whole experience of going to court traumatic and alienating'. 'Court proceedings do not appear.... to improve parental relationships and therefore their capacity to manage post-separation parenting.'[58] Researchers at the University of East Anglia concluded that 'existing legal interventions have limited capacity to facilitate contact or reverse a

53 See note 18.
54 Neale and Wade (n 36) 32.
55 Ibid 36.
56 FJYPB video shown at the conference of the Family Mediators Association 2020.
57 Trinder, L, 'Conciliation, the Private Law Programme and Children's Well-being' [2008] *Family Law* 338, 341.
58 Hunt, J, *Parental Perspectives on the Family Justice System in England and Wales: a review of research*, Report for the Family Justice Council, December 2009, 118 and 121.

downward spiral in contact relationships. Resources should be redirected to more creative work on improving parental relationships.'[59]

Mediation focuses on improving parental relationships. Follow-up studies indicate that mediation reduces conflict between separated parents, helps to resolve issues and increases co-operation over children. A three-year study at the University of Newcastle found that 'reaching agreements through mediation is a vital component in making and maintaining co-operative relationships between separated parents.'[60] A Ministry of Justice Green Paper[61] reported in 2010 that 'the full and partial success rate of publicly funded mediations now stands at 70% (with the full resolution of cases accounting for 66% of this)'. A survey of FMC members in 2019 found that if each parent (or other family member) attended a MIAM, 73% accepted mediation and the same percentage of mediation participants reached full or partial agreement.[62] Emery's study in the US used a control group to compare the outcomes of mediation and court proceedings over a 12-year period. Non-resident parents in the mediated group were found to have much more contact with their children and be much more involved in their children's lives than parents who litigated. 30% of non-resident parents who used mediation said they saw their children weekly or more often, compared with 8% of parents who litigated and 54% said they talked to their children once a week or more, compared with 13% who litigated.[63] The Mapping Paths to Family Justice Study[64] reported that almost three quarters of participants in mediation said they had valued the structure that mediation provided, while just over half said they were satisfied with the outcome. However, some women who had met with a male mediator had felt disadvantaged, or not well understood, and a third said they were dissatisfied, having compromised or capitulated to protect their children or avoid court proceedings. Since the Mapping Paths study, further training and guidelines have been provided for mediators to develop their awareness and skills in assessing suitability and readiness for mediation and in addressing power imbalances. In a more recent study, the Mapping Paths researchers found that children's messages and suggestions helped parents to communicate better and agree arrangements, while children say that talking with a mediator boosted their self-esteem and helped them to feel better.[65] These significant findings are discussed in the final chapter.

59 Trinder Beek and Connolly (n 6) 092, 1.

60 McCarthy, P and Walker, J, *The longer-term impact of family mediation* (Joseph Rowntree Findings, 1996) 103, 1.

61 Ministry of Justice Green Paper, *Legal Aid Reform 2010*, para 4.71.

62 Family Mediation Council Survey of Members, January 2020.

63 Emery, R et al., 'Child Custody Mediation and Litigation: Custody, Contact and Co-parenting twelve years after initial dispute resolution' (2001) 69(2) *Journal of Consulting and Clinical Psychology* 323–32.

64 Barlow, Hunter, Smithson and Ewing, *Mapping Paths to Family Justice – Briefing Paper and Report on Key Findings* (Universities of Exeter and Kent, June 2014) 12.

65 University of Exeter Wellcome Centre, Healthy Relationships Project, *Report and Key Findings*, March 2022.

Chapter 12

Children's resilience and the benefits of talking with a mediator

'Resilience Factors'

Research studies referred to in the previous chapter indicate that some children's negative experiences during and following their parents' separation may result in behavioural problems and mental health issues, whereas other children may do very well. What makes the difference? Is it nature, nurture or both? The answer may lie in what scientists call 'resilience factors'. Schaefer[1] describes resilience as a dynamic process, rather than as an inherited trait. Rutter, a well-known writer on resilience, explains that

> 'it matters greatly how people deal with adversities and life stressors – perhaps not so much in the particular coping strategy employed, but in the fact that they do *act* and not simply react. ...The promotion of resilience does not lie in an avoidance of stress, but rather in encountering stress at a time and in a way that allows self-confidence and social competence to increase through mastery and appropriate responsibility.'[2]

Scientists studying mental health resilience in the wake of childhood adversity are examining how the brain reacts to stress, the importance of a 'time window' and the need for a 'complexity science' approach. Complexity science recognises that there is not a single mechanism that determines whether a person is resilient or not, but rather a range of interrelated factors that change over time. With the current high rates of mental health issues among young people, particularly following periods of lockdown during the Covid-19 pandemic, we need to understand how to increase young people's resilience during their transition from childhood to adulthood. NHS statistics show that the number of children and young people undergoing or awaiting treatment for mental health issues increased from 24% in 2020 to 54% in 2022.[3] 'Depression, anxiety and conduct disorder (a type of behavioural problem) are often a direct result of what is happening in their lives.'[4] When children lack information, explanations and reassurance, their anxiety and distress increase.[5]

---

1 Schaefer et al., 'The health-related functions of social support' (1981) 4(4) *Journal of Behavioural Medicine* 381–406.
2 Rutter, M, 'Resilience in the Face of Adversity' (1985) 147 *British Journal of Psychiatry* 608.
3 Young Minds, NHS Digital, April 2022.
4 Mental Health Foundation website, updated 12 August 2021.
5 Fortin, J et al., 'Taking a Longer View of Contact – the perspectives of young adults who experienced parental separation in their youth January' [2013] *Family Law* 104.

During adolescence, major changes take place in the brain and these changes, together with hormonal changes, make young people more vulnerable to the risk of developing mental disorders and/or behavioural difficulties. Professor Van Hamelen, Professor of Brain Safety and Resilience at the University of Cambridge, explains that resilience functioning is aided by what are called 'resilience factors', some of which are physiological, such as genetic make-up and the brain's reaction to stress, whereas other factors depend on social intervention and support.[6] One study carried out by Professor Van Hamelin and her Cambridge group found that adolescents who had positive relationships with a number of friends showed higher levels of resilience than those with few friends, while another study found that the ability to recall positive memories was a buffering factor that reduced the risk of mental illness. The researchers report that the period around 14 years of age seems particularly critical, when developing regions of the brain are vulnerable to stress. Intervention and social support during this 'time window' are particularly important.

Children with low self-esteem tend to feel powerless to change their circumstances. Self-esteem is a very important resilience factor that comes not only from positive attachments, but also from taking part in activities, experiencing success and acting in a helpful, caring and responsible way.[7] 'Hanna' was adopted when she was a year old. When she was four years old, her adoptive parents separated and then divorced. Hanna remained living with her adoptive mother and mediation took place over contact arrangements with her adoptive father, which had been resisted by her mother. Hanna's mother was a nurse and when she worked nights, Hanna was left at home on her own. Her father remarried and he and his second wife had two daughters whom Hanna regarded as her younger sisters. As a teenager, when staying with her mother, Hanna began to stay out late at night and at the age of 15, she ran away and was found living with her boyfriend's family and expecting a baby. She was taken into the care of the local authority and placed in a residential home. Hanna was allowed to keep her baby and when she left care, she and her baby daughter were rehoused by the local authority. Hanna ended her relationship with her boyfriend and after refusing contact with both adoptive parents for a time, she began to visit each of them again of her own volition. She managed well as a single parent, caring for her daughter, working full-time and visiting her adoptive father, his new partner and their teenage daughters. Her adoptive father's steady support and her relationships with him and her half-sisters were lifelines that helped Hanna to grow her self-esteem and overcome earlier difficulties in becoming a caring and responsible parent herself.

The role of ChiM in increasing children's resilience

When asked in a study what they thought made for a happy life, children identified as their top priorities feeling loved, having good relationships with family and friends and having someone to talk to and rely on. '[Love means] people who care about you, family and friends, because then they'll be there for you when you're upset.'[8] Children said that being able to express themselves without being

6 'Resilience – a complexity science approach' Professor Anne-Laura Van Harmelen – 'In Conversation' – ACAMH.

7 Daniel, B, Wassell, S and Gilligan, R, 'It's just common sense, isn't it? Exploring ways of putting the theory of resilience into action (1999) 23(3) *Adoption and Fostering*.

8 Children's views on well-being and what makes a happy life, UK: 2020 – Office for National Statistics (ons.gov.uk).

judged by others was crucial for their well-being. Studies referred to in previous chapters emphasise the importance for young people of having the opportunity to talk to someone they can trust, especially during a family crisis or transition when decisions are being made that affect their lives. Their parents may be less accessible at this time, because they are preoccupied with their own troubles. The opportunity to talk with a qualified family mediator during a crucial 'time window' in a child's development acts as a resilience factor which enables the child's 'self-confidence and social competence to increase through mastery and appropriate responsibility.'[9] 'The child's relationship with his or her parents is the crucible for learning about other people'.[10]

One of the first studies of children's experience of talking with a mediator was carried out in Scotland. Although the children said they had felt uncertain initially, almost all of those who talked with a mediator spoke positively about their experience.[11] They reported:

- Feeling 'relieved', 'much easier', less anxious about being pulled between their parents.
- Better communication between the children and their parents.
- Better contact arrangements and feeling happier about contact visits.
- More understanding of their situation ('we like going to dad's now that we understand more' said an eight-year-old girl, speaking for herself and her sister).
- Having the opportunity to express their feelings. One teenager said she had not previously spoken to anyone about how she was feeling and she now felt that she and her parents understood each other better.
- Realising they were not alone in having these feelings.
- Asking the mediator's help to convey a message to their parents or make requests, such as making phone calls to an absent parent.
- Borrowing books to help them understand what was happening.
- Being able to keep out of issues between parents that did not concern them.

Nearly all the children interviewed (24 out of 28) felt they had definitely benefited from seeing the mediator. The remaining four said that everything was all right anyway, so it had not made much difference.

Exeter University research findings on children's participation in mediation

An evaluation of the DWP-funded Mediation in Mind project[12] by researchers at the University of Exeter provides further evidence that taking account of children's

9 Rutter (n 2) above.
10 Baron-Cohen, S, *Zero Degrees of Empathy* (Penguin Books, 2011) 52.
11 Garwood, F, *Children in Conciliation* 1989, Scottish Association of Family Conciliation Services.
12 Barlow, A, and Ewing, J, *An Evaluation of 'Mediation in Mind,* Final Report, University of Exeter, June 2020.

views and concerns encourages parents to co-operate and improves father-child relationships. The study found that children who were consulted over arrangements were happier than those who were not consulted.

In 2022, the Exeter researchers published a further study which provided the first qualitative research findings on children's participation in mediation in England and Wales.[13] In the first phase of the study, a systematic review was undertaken of relationship support programmes for young people aged 11 to 18, with the aim of developing effective 'support for young people to become resilient adults capable of making positive choices and maintaining happy, health-promoting intimate relationships.'[14] The second and third phases explored the perspectives of young people on relationship education and gathered the views of relationship professionals. Before embarking on the fourth phase, the researchers ran two focus groups with members of the Family Justice Young People's Board (FJYPB) to seek their views on young people's information and support needs following parental separation. Max, a member of the FJYPB, said: 'I think the child should be involved as much as they can, just because it's their life that's being decided about. You should [not] let your parents decide … what's going to happen in your life … because it's not their life they are making decisions for.'

The fourth phase of the study included Interviews with a sample of 20 young people, ranging in age from 9 to 19, who had talked with a family mediator. There were also sample groups consisting of 12 parents (five fathers and seven mothers) and 20 ChiM-trained family mediators from all five FMC member organisations. The young people said they had been unaware of their right to be heard under the UNCRC 1989, but considered it a matter of principle that their voice should be heard. Almost all of the 20 parents in the sample told the researchers that they had taken account of their children's wishes and views and had reached agreement on child arrangements without going to court. One father had rejected the wishes of his two children to have more say in contact arrangements. His children were deeply disappointed. It is important to confirm parents' willingness to listen to their children's messages and consider their views and wishes, before the children are invited to talk. But even when their wishes are not followed, young people say that talking to an empathetic listener helps them to feel better. Alfie said: 'It opened me a lot more and made me a lot more confident to speak to my parents about things, which just made a lot of stuff much, much easier and took a lot of stress off my chest.'[15]

Summary of the Exeter study on young people's views and experience of ChiM

- Young people want a voice in the decision-making process about arrangements when their parents separate.
- Young people and professionals strongly support the inclusion of children's rights when parents separate in the RE curriculum, given the large numbers affected.

13 University of Exeter, *The_Healthy_Relationships_Project_Report_-and_Key_Findings.pdf*, March 2022.
14 Ibid, Background and Aims, 3.
15 Ibid, 12.

- Young people feel they are more resilient in handling issues than adults give them credit for.
- Having your voice heard as a young person in parental mediation is empowering and cathartic, bringing mental health and well-being benefits.
- Giving young people a forum in which they can talk and be heard is the most helpful thing you can do when parents separate.
- Speaking to an empathetic third party is an opportunity for children to discuss things they felt unable to raise with their parents, enabling them to offload their concerns and reduce their anxieties.
- Inclusion in mediation signalled parents cared about their opinions, helped them understand options and improved communication between children and parents.

The ChiM mediators who were interviewed had an average of 16 years' experience in talking with children and young people in mediation. The mediators reported that conflict between parents was reduced when they understood their children's concerns and taking account of the concerns encouraged parents to cooperate and avoid or discontinue court proceedings. Young people who spoke to the researchers were very positive about their experience of talking with a mediator online. One boy said it was easier to see his siblings' faces on the screen in a Zoom meeting than in an office environment and that it was good to see how they were feeling.[16]

The researchers referred to the barriers to ChiM which they had identified in their previous Mapping Paths study.[17] These included low awareness among parents of children's opportunity and right to participate, additional costs, and reluctance to involve children in what parents regard as adult issues. Another barrier was mediators' lack of confidence in having the skills to talk with children and young people who may be caught in very difficult and distressing situations. Informal feedback from mediators indicates increasing confidence. One mediator has reported doing two mediation meetings per week, on average, in which she talks with the children concerned. This is an account of another mediator's first meeting with a child:

> 'It was truly amazing and left me with goose bumps all over at the power of the children's voices. The transformation of the way the parents behaved compared to the previous week was astonishing – once they saw their children's handwriting with messages for them on the flip-chart they became totally child focussed and stopped bickering. Wow! The children were so sweet and I felt privileged that they felt safe to open their hearts to me as they did. They came out with some cracking lines as well – the little 7 year old girl was not sure at first if she wanted her parents to have feedback, then she said: 'I have never kept secrets from my Mummy and Daddy before, so I am not about to start'. The parents e-mailed to thank me and said they both felt it had really helped their

16 Ewing, J, (2020) *The Healthy Relationships Transitions (HeaRT) Project: Child-inclusive mediation – overcoming barriers to greater uptake*, Family Mediators Association Annual Conference, *Mediating in a Time of Change*. Online 30 September 2020.

17 Barlow, A et al., *Mapping Paths to Family Justice – Briefing Paper and Report on Key Findings* (Universities of Exeter and Kent, June 2014).

children. They said that their communications were much improved and the benefits to the children were clear.'[18]

Australian research on hearing the voice of the child during mediation

In Australia, children whose parents are taking part in mediation are referred to a child consultant, who talks with the child without having had a prior meeting with the parents, and gives feedback to the parents in a subsequent mediation meeting on the child's position and feelings. The child consultant then withdraws, leaving the mediator to continue working with the parents. This approach, developed by Dr Jenn McIntosh and her colleagues, is described as a 'brief, single-session assessment followed by a therapeutic dialogue between child specialist, parents, and mediator about the adjustment and developmental needs of each child and the implications of this for parenting plans.'[19] The child consultant seeks to understand the child's needs and feelings, helping younger children to talk while drawing pictures or playing with a dolls' house. The child may be invited to choose small dolls to represent members of their family, including themselves. After meeting with the child, the consultant joins a mediation meeting and advises the parents on the child's needs and concerns, possibly illustrated by the child's drawing or painting. After giving feedback and encouraging the parents to co-operate, the child specialist withdraws and the mediation continues. Child specialists are experts trained in play therapy and in understanding non-verbal, as well as verbal, communications from children. The role of a child specialist who interprets a child's play or pictures and provides guidance to parents differs from the role of a ChiM mediator who facilitates communication between children and parents, without giving opinions or offering advice. Another difference is that the Australian system is funded by the State and provided by well-resourced family centres.

The great majority (86%) of children who took part in a follow-up study said they had found it helpful to talk to the child consultant. One child said: 'It helped to have someone listen to what I said, for it to be confidential, but also she would pass on to my parents what I wanted them to know. I was allowed to speak and say what I want. I could speak about problems. Afterwards I felt really good, like much better.' Another child said: 'He [child consultant] helped a lot, he helped get the sadness away from me.'[20] The researchers concluded that talking with a child consultant 'offered children a safe, specialist, avenue for their views and needs to be considered and indeed to impact significantly upon the way in which their parents were able to resolve their parenting disputes'.[21]

McIntosh and her colleagues 'compared outcomes over one year of two groups of separated parents who attended two different forms of brief therapeutic mediation for entrenched parenting disputes. The two interventions each targeted psychological resolution of parental conflict, enhanced parental reflective

18 With thanks to Jacqueline Gregory (also quoted in Parkinson, *Family Mediation* 2020, 224).
19 McIntosh, Smyth, Wells and Long, 'Child-Focused and Child-Inclusive Divorce Mediation: Comparative Outcomes' (2008) 46(1) *Family Courts Review* (Association of Family and Conciliation Courts) 122.
20 Ibid.
21 Ibid.

function and reduced distress for their children.'[22] In child-focused mediation, parents are encouraged to consider their children's needs without the children participating directly, whereas when children participate directly, their views and feelings are shared with their parents, who are helped to understand and consider their concerns. In the year following mediation, the researchers found a lasting reduction of conflict and improved management of disputes in both groups. In the group in which children participated, improved relationships were more evident, particularly between fathers and children, and there were more noticeable benefits in children's developmental recovery from high-conflict separation. Agreements reached were significantly more durable. The parents in this group were only half as likely as parents in the child-focused group to instigate further litigation on child arrangements. At the IVth World Mediation Conference held in Buenos Aires in May 2003, Alan Campbell, a child consultant from Australia, observed that 'the inclusion of children in mediation recognises their status as human beings in their own right and provides them with a forum where their views can be appropriately considered.'[23]

Argentina

A research study on the use of child-inclusive mediation in the Bahía Blanca region of Argentina is being carried out by two mediators, both from a legal background. Elstein and Felibert follow the same principles as those used in the UK: inviting the child's participation, providing confidentiality (unless safeguarding is needed), maintaining impartiality and encouraging parents or carers to consider the child's views and suggestions in reaching their decisions. Elstein and Felibert also offer similar options for children and young people to take part – with their parents, alone, and/or with siblings. They give examples of outcomes, such as a mediation in which a boy, previously unwilling to see his father, told his mother that after talking with the mediators he felt ready to see his father the following Sunday. In another mediation, a teenage girl asked the mediator to tell her father that she would contact him to suggest going out somewhere together. Elstein and Felibert conclude that 'the simple, yet profound, perspective offered by children and young people in mediation is indispensable in informing the decisions that are being taken by their parents or carers'.[24]

Norway

Norway has a mandatory system of child-inclusive mediation, similar to the Australian system in being part of a statutory process, rather than a voluntary process offered to separating couples and family members who have matters needing settlement. Attendance at a one-hour mediation session is mandatory in Norway for all separating/separated/divorcing spouses or cohabiting partners who have children under the age of 16. Further mediation sessions can be arranged if required, up to a maximum of seven hours. Children are systematically included because 'separation and divorce are recognised as one of the important contexts

22 Ibid 105.
23 Campbell, A, *Listening to children – child-inclusive mediation practice*, paper given at the IVth World Mediation Conference, Buenos Aires, May 2003.
24 Elstein, S and Felibert, M, *Listening to Children in Mediation*, May 2023, La Trama, Buenos Aires revistalatrama.com.ar (quotation translated by the author).

in which children must be heard'.[25] After talking with the parents, the mediator talks with the child alone, or with siblings together. The parents then rejoin the meeting and the mediator shares messages from the children, expressed as closely as possible in the child's own words. Parents retain their responsibility for decisions and if they are unable to reach agreement after the children have been heard, the mediation continues without the children being present. Researchers in Norway found that children's participation in mediation influenced parents' decisions and that there was no evidence that including children in mediation had any adverse consequences. In a follow-up study,[26] children were asked to complete a questionnaire and 345 children (97%) answered one or more questions. 86% said they had liked talking with the mediator and 92% said they had felt well understood. One child wrote: 'Hard to share ourselves equally. Everyday life is very busy, don't want 50/50.'

International cross-border mediation

The Guide to International Family Mediation produced by International Social Service can be downloaded from the ISS website in a number of languages, free of charge.[27] The Guide recognises the child's right to be heard, with quotations from parents and children with experience of cross-border mediation. Alexander, aged 11, said: 'I knew that my parents loved me. The mediator helped me tell my parents that I did not want to decide and that really lifted a weight off my chest.' Justin, aged 14, said: 'I was able to tell the two of them what I had in my heart and that I wanted to get to know my father (who had been away for eight years).'[28] The Guide refers to the growing evidence that taking part in mediation benefits children and young people and increases parents' understanding of their views and feelings.

Groups for children experiencing parental separation

In France, 'Groupes de Paroles' and in Italy, 'Gruppi di Parola', are arranged for children of separated parents. Groups for children of different ages, led by family mediators, are arranged in four sessions, each lasting two hours. The children are helped to express their feelings through talking, playing games and drawing pictures and find it very helpful to realise they are not alone. They are encouraged to compose a joint letter to their parents, explaining what they would like their parents to understand better in general, without needing to worry about how their own parents would react to an individual letter. The group letter is shared with their parents collectively and the parents respond as a group. A research study at the Catholic University of Milan studied videotapes (made with the written consent of parents and children) of 20 groups involving 113 children aged from 6–12. The researchers found that the children found it very helpful to share their

25 United Nations General Comment No 12, 2009, points 50 and 52.
26 Thørnblad and Strandbu, 'The Involvement of Children in the Process of Mandatory Family Mediation' in Nylund et al. (eds), *Nordic Mediation Research* (Springer Books, 2018) 183–208.
27 Caratsch, C, *Resolving Family Conflicts – a Guide to International Family Mediation,* International Social Service, Geneva, 2014.
28 Ibid 43.

experiences and feelings and to develop ideas on how to cope better and help each other. Their letters made a powerful impact on parents, increasing parents' understanding of their children's experience and leading to changes in parents' behaviour and in their arrangements for their children.[29] Bringing children together to share their experiences and feelings and construct a communal letter to their parents is described as a process of convergence, beginning when parents register their children for the group and completing the circle when parents respond to their children's questions and messages.[30]

Resilience in opening up new avenues of communication

Research findings in the UK and other countries show consistently that the participation of children and young people in mediation provides significant benefits for them, and also for their parents and carers. Child-parent relationships are strengthened, communication in the family becomes freer and arrangements work better. Mediators, parents and those who work with children and young people need knowledge of brain development in order to understand, for example, why risk-taking is heightened in adolescence. Adolescents are susceptible to peer group pressure and hypersensitive to being socially excluded, but they are also responsive to new opportunities. Our brains are plastic at all ages, but during adolescence, when neuroplasticity in certain brain regions is heightened, interventions such as mediation can increase a young person's resilience and creativity.

Danny aged nine and Max aged seven

Danny, aged nine, and Max, aged seven, told their parents that they wanted to meet the mediator too. Their parents gave consent and the mediator talked with the boys together, then separately and finally together again. Danny told the mediator: 'I wrote out my agenda last night.' He then went through his agenda, ticking off each item as he went. Each boy wrote out a message for their parents. Max needed a little help, but he could write very well for his age. He took a great liking to the book, *Dinosaurs Divorce*.[31] He looked at the drawing of a dinosaur mother scolding her dinosaur child and read aloud the thought bubble saying 'Parents sometimes fight with you when really they are angry with each other!' 'EXACTLY!' exclaimed Max: 'I need a copy of this book at my mum's house and a copy at my dad's house as well'. When his mother asked Max later whether talking to the mediator had helped, he said: 'It helped to take away the pain in my tummy.' The mother also reported that 'Danny looks like the weight of the world has been lifted off his shoulders. He has started a new list of things he would like to discuss with you. It's fantastic he can speak to someone he can trust.'

29 Marzotto (ed), *Gruppi di parola per figli di genitori separati* (Vita e Pensiero, 2010).
30 Bonadotta, M and Farinacci, P, 'Ascoltare I figli di separati nei Gruppi di Parola' in Bramanti and Marzotto (eds), *Ascoltare lasciando traccia* (Vita e Pensiero, 2019).
31 Brown and Brown, *Dinosaurs Divorce – A Guide for Changing Families* (Dino Life Guides, 1988).

Outside the realm of mediation, there are well-known examples of young people who overcame adversity through their own determination and who, with strong support from their family and friends, became champions of a particular cause. Malala Yousafzai, aged 17, was campaigning for Pakistani girls to have the right to education when she was shot in the head by the Taliban. After a long recovery in a London hospital, Malala continued to campaign for girls' education and the rights of women. She graduated from Oxford University and in 2014, Malala was awarded the Nobel Peace Prize, the youngest ever recipient.[32] At the age of 15, Greta Thunberg began sitting outside the Swedish Parliament every Friday, with a placard calling for action on climate change. Greta had previously suffered from a severe eating disorder and had been diagnosed as having Asperger's syndrome, which, rather than seeing as a disability, Greta regards as her 'superpower'. Greta held up a sign saying 'School Strike for Climate' and other students soon joined her under the banner of 'Fridays for Future.' In 2019, there were strikes in many cities, each involving over a million students. Greta had the courage to rebuke the United Nations Climate Change Conference (COP25) and the European Parliament for their failure to take action on the climate crisis. In 2019, she was included in the Forbes list of the world's 100 Most Powerful Women.

Max Woosey, aged ten, raised funds for his neighbour's cancer treatment by sleeping in a tent in his garden every night for three years. Max raised more than £700,000 for a local hospice and provided funding for 15 nurses' salaries for a year. Max said: 'Kids can play a huge role in society. Look at Greta Thunberg. She's an inspiration.'

32 Yousafzai, M, *I Am Malala* (Phoenix, 2013).

Appendix A

Including children and young people in mediation – a handout for parents and carers

Family mediation helps families to agree arrangements for children and financial matters without the delays and costs of going to court. An information and assessment meeting (MIAM) with a qualified family mediator is offered to each participant separately, often online, to explain how mediation works and to understand what needs to be settled. The mediator checks for any concerns, particularly about domestic abuse, coercive control and safeguarding of children. If mediation is suitable and accepted by the participants, they are invited to sign an Agreement to Mediate, which explains that the mediator is impartial and mediation is voluntary and confidential, except where a child is in need of safeguarding or there are concerns about someone who may be at risk of harm. The mediator helps participants to reach their own decisions, without advising on the terms of settlement or providing solutions.

Children's needs and well-being

Mediators seek the views of parents and carers on their children's needs and best interests and explain that children and young people who are able to express their views, and who wish to do so, have the right to be consulted. A study with young adults whose parents separated during their childhood found that most of them thought their parents had managed their separation well. Many of them said, however, that they had wanted to talk to someone about their position and feelings – someone they could trust, who was not making judgments or writing a report about them – but they had not had a chance to do so. Young people want to be involved in working out arrangements and the great majority say they want the chance to talk and offer their ideas and suggestions.

Talking to someone they trust helps children and young people to feel better

Parents often think that children should not be involved in adult matters and that including them in mediation will cause them anxiety. However, children and young people who accept the invitation to talk with a qualified family mediator told a researcher afterwards that they found it very helpful. They said it was a great relief to be able to talk freely and decide what they would like their parents to understand and take into account in making arrangements for them. Feedback from parents was very positive too. Parents said that communication in the family had become easier and that their children's ideas and suggestions helped them to agree arrangements that worked well. Researchers have found that talking with a mediator has mental health benefits for children and young people. They can talk with the mediator online or meet in person, as they prefer.

Will the child be told what to say?

Some parents fear that the other parent will coach the child on what to say to the mediator and that the child will be unable to express their true feelings. Parents are asked to sign a written undertaking that they will not coach their child on what to say to the mediator, or question or scold the child afterwards about what the child said. The mediator explains to children and young people that their parents have made these promises and that the child or young person is not being asked to make choices or decisions.

Sharing children's messages with their parents and carers

When young people have a conversation with a mediator and decide the message and suggestions that they would like their parents to consider, they are asked whether they would like to share their message with their parents themselves, either at home, or in a family meeting with the mediator's support, or whether they would like the mediator to share their message with their parents. Sometimes a child resists contact with their father or mother and the parents often blame each other. But when the child or young person talks with a mediator, they may explain something which, from the parents' point of view, seems quite a minor problem that they can deal with, when they understand what it is. At other times, there may be more deep-rooted problems. When parents listen and respond to their children in helpful and reassuring ways, there can be a turning-point which reduces conflict and has long-term benefits for children's development and mental health.

Communication in the family becomes easier when children have an opportunity to talk with a qualified family mediator.

What about the cost?

A limited amount of legal aid for mediation is available for those who qualify. The Mediation Voucher Scheme currently provides £500 worth of mediation on child-related matters for those paying privately. This funding may not be sufficient to cover additional meetings but a court application is likely to cost more. it can take a year to obtain a child arrangements order and a court order may not work as well in practice as arrangements made by parents and children themselves.

What do children say about talking with a specially trained family mediator?

'I think I can explain it to my mum myself now, but please would you explain it too?'

'Just tell my parents that I know they're doing their best.'

'If we stay at Dad's on Wednesday nights we'll be late for school on Thursday and I don't want to miss the maths class. I'm top in maths.'

'Talking about my worries helped to take away the pain in my tummy.'

'I feel clearer about things now.'

'I'd like us all to meet as a family before next Christmas to work out what we're doing.'

'It's my life too.'

Appendix B

Draft code of practice for child-inclusive mediation

Mediators' duties and responsibilities regarding children's welfare and safety

Mediators must at all times have particular regard to the welfare and well-being of any children of the family and should encourage participants to focus on their children's needs and best interests, as well as on their own.[1]

Safeguarding of children at risk

At the information and assessment meeting (MIAM) and throughout the mediation process, mediators must check for any indications or concerns regarding any form of abuse, or risk of harm, to a child or vulnerable adult. Where there are indications or concerns that a child may be at risk of harm and in need of safeguarding, the mediator must enquire whether these concerns have been reported and if so, when, by whom and to whom, and whether a child protection service is currently involved. Irrespective of whether a participant has reported concerns, the mediator must refer the matter to the duty social worker without delay.[2]

Where the social worker finds insufficient grounds to warrant a child protection order or other action, the social worker may recommend that mediation should continue, if the participants are willing to resume the mediation. Alternatively, the participants should be advised to seek advice and help from an appropriate agency.

Children in Mediation (ChiM)

When mediation has been considered at initial information and assessment meetings and found to be safe and suitable, participants must sign the Agreement to Mediate before mediation takes place and before any meeting with children.

Where there are children in the family, mediators must encourage participants to consider the children's wishes and feelings. Children of sufficient maturity who are

1 Family Mediation Council Code of Practice revised 2018, s 5.3.
2 FMC Code of Practice for Family Mediation 2018, s 5.5.3.

able to express their views and wishes should be offered the opportunity to have their voices heard directly during the mediation, if they wish.[3] At initial information and mediation meetings and in mediation, mediators should explain the child's right to have a voice, if the child wishes, and encourage parents to consider ways in which the child's voice may be heard.

The mediator should enquire whether any other professional, such as a psychologist or school counsellor, is seeing the child or working with the family, in order to avoid a duplication of roles and responsibilities where the child is concerned. If a social worker or other child expert is involved, the parents or carers should be asked to agree to the mediator liaising with the professional concerned, to establish whether mediation would be appropriate.

Definition of child-inclusive mediation (ChiM)

Child-inclusive mediation provides opportunities for children and young people to have their voice heard directly during the process of mediation, to help them feel respected and listened to and, at their request, to assist parents or carers to receive, understand and take account of the child's messages and/or suggestions regarding decisions and arrangements for the child.[4]

Core principles

1 Voluntary participation

The participation of the child or young person requires the informed consent of both parents, or those holding parental responsibility. The child or young person is offered the opportunity to express their views and wishes and is free to accept or decline the invitation. The courts do not have power to order the child's participation.

2 Confidentiality

Conversations with a child or young person in mediation are confidential and are not reportable to the court or to third parties, except where there are safeguarding and child protection concerns.

The child or young person may request the mediator to share a message or suggestions with their parents in the child's own words, without adding further information or interpretation. The confidential and legally privileged Mediation Summary may refer to the *fact* that the child or young person talked with the mediator and that their views and wishes were taken into account by their parents or carers, but the Summary must not report the *content* of what the child said to the mediator. However, while this Summary is both confidential and legally privileged, participants, preferably after taking independent legal advice, may give their joint

3 Adapted from s 6.6.1.
4 Family Mediation Council Code of Practice, s 6.6.1.

written consent to waive their confidentiality, so that the Mediation Summary may be made available to the court to facilitate the making of a consent order.

Young people sometimes bring a handwritten letter or notes to show the mediator, saying that they wish this written expression of their wishes and concerns to be made available to the court, as well as to their parents. Under the UN Convention on the Rights of the Child 1989, to which the UK is a signatory, a young person of sufficient maturity has the right to have their voice heard, if they wish, in proceedings that concern them. Where a parent or carer has applied for a child arrangements order and court proceedings are underway, the mediator should make the young person's letter or notes available to the court, without providing further information, and should notify the parents accordingly.

3 Impartiality of the mediator

Mediators must maintain their impartiality in talking with a child or young person and should remain neutral regarding the outcome of the mediation, except where a child might be at risk of harm. The mediator's role is to facilitate communication and encourage co-operation between family members, without acting as the child's advocate or representative, or becoming aligned with a parent or with a child. The mediator should not give advice, express opinions or steer participants towards an outcome favoured by the mediator.

4 Decisions remain with the child's parents/those holding parental responsibility

Mediators must take care not to raise a child's hopes of achieving the solution they are hoping for, or to feel in any way responsible for the outcome. Children and young people may make requests and offer suggestions, but they are not asked to make choices and they do not carry responsibility for decisions. Their parents or guardians are encouraged to take account of their children's views and suggestions in reaching their decisions.

Pre-requisites for ChiM

1. Mediators who talk with children and young people during the process of mediation must be specifically trained and recognised to do so, having completed successfully a training programme in ChiM recognised by the Family Mediation Council (FMC).
2. Where safety checks permitted by law are necessary to confirm the mediator's eligibility to meet with children, ChiM mediators must have completed these safety checks.
3. The mediator must have an additional professional practice consultant (PPC) who is qualified in ChiM, if their current PPC is not ChiM-qualified, for regular case discussion and for guidance in challenging ChiM cases.
4. Mediators who meet with a child in person, rather than online, must have suitable rooms and facilities where children and young people are safe at all times and can feel comfortable and at ease. The mediator should consider

having a co-mediator or colleague who is available to co-mediate, or observe, a meeting with a child or young person, as a safeguard against the possibility of an allegation being made against the mediator.

5 Before a child or young person is invited to talk with a ChiM-qualified mediator, parents/carers must be taking part in mediation and must give their written consent in which they confirm their willingness to receive and consider their child's views and wishes and give undertakings that they will not coach the child on what to say to the mediator, nor question or reproach the child afterwards. Where the child has a parent or legal guardian who is not a participant in the mediation, this person's consent to the child's participation should also be sought.

6 When parents or carers agree that their child or children should have the opportunity to talk and express their views and feelings, different options should be explored, such as talking with the same mediator, if ChiM-qualified, or with a different, ChiM-qualified mediator, online, or in an in-person meeting, with siblings together and/or separately. There may be a short family meeting initially for introductions, and also afterwards, if the child wishes to give their message to their parents themselves, with the mediator's support, or to be present when the mediator gives it.

7 With the consent of both parents/carers, the mediator may contact the child or young person directly, to invite them to have a talk, either online, or come to an in-person meeting, if they prefer. If the conversation with the child or young person takes place online, the mediator needs to be alert for any sign that someone else is present with the child. To check that nobody else is in the room, the mediator may ask the child to move the camera around to show their room and their favourite things.

8 The mediator should maintain a checklist on file, recording pre-requisites that were met and file notes for reference. Mediators should not provide reports, notes or written feedback to parents or third parties.

9 The mediator should provide a confidential summary of the outcome that parents are asked to share with their child, or, if mediation is ongoing, an interim summary, or a letter from the mediator to the child, approved by the parents.

10 In order to extend their knowledge and develop their skills, the mediator must undertake the required number of hours of continuing ChiM-specific training, as currently laid down by the FMC.

A staged process

ChiM is a process, not a one-off event. This process needs to be planned and structured carefully in a series of stages. A single conversation with a child or young person may not be sufficient. The mediator should leave the door open for a further talk with the child, if the child wishes to come again. Children may think afterwards of something else they wanted to say, or they may have second thoughts, or the situation may change. It should therefore be explained to children at the initial meeting that they are welcome to have a further talk, if they wish, but their parents' consent would need to be re-confirmed first.

Appendix C

Parental consent for a meeting with a child or young person (example of mediator's letter to parents)

....

Dear .... and...............

I am glad that you would like ..... (child or children) to have the opportunity to come and talk with [......] about how things are going and, if they wish, decide a message or make a suggestion about arrangements that they would like you to consider. Young people say it helps them to talk and be listened to. Sometimes there is just a small thing they are concerned about which they haven't mentioned to you, because they did not want to bother you with it.

[The plan is that [........] will meet with them together first of all, and then have a chat with each of them separately, as siblings can have different views and ideas.]

........will be invited to come ...... on the understanding that:-

1 The purpose of the conversation is to give .... the opportunity to talk about their views and feelings and put forward suggestions or requests that she/he/they think would help arrangements to work as well as possible for all of you. I shall not ask .... to make any choices or decisions and it will be clear that you will be responsible as their parents for decisions and arrangements.

2 You confirm that you will not tell.....what they should or shouldn't say, and that you will not reproach them afterwards or ask them questions about what they said or didn't say, as this would make them anxious and might make it more difficult for them to explain things to you in the future.

3 You understand that even if .... does not have any messages that they wish to be shared with you, having the chance to talk and contribute their views and ideas benefits children and helps them to feel better.

4 The conversation with .... will be confidential, except where there is any indication that a child is in need of safeguarding, in which case this must be referred to the child protection service for further enquiry.

5 [name of children] will be asked whether they have a message, suggestion or request that they would like to share with you. If so, they will be asked to write it down, or they can ask the mediator to write it down for them in their own

words. They may like to share their messages with you in a family meeting with the mediator present, or they can ask the mediator to share their messages with you on your own, without adding an opinion or more information.

6 You confirm that you are willing to listen to.....'s message and take their views into account in reaching your decisions and making arrangements.

I should be grateful if you would both sign this letter to confirm that you accept the understandings set out above and that you would like an invitation to be sent to ......

If....... accepts the invitation and would like to talk with the mediator in person, rather than online, ... (father/mother or both parents) will bring them to the meeting and pick them up afterwards.

I look forward very much to the pleasure of meeting .... and talking with her/him/them.

Yours sincerely

[Accredited family mediator qualified to meet with children and young people]

We agree to ...... (mediator) meeting with ...... (our children) on the conditions set out above.

.... Signature of parent

.... Name of parent

Date......................................

.... Signature of parent

.... Name of parent

Date......................................

Appendix D

Sample letter inviting a child or young person to meet with the mediator

Dear

My name is .... and as I think you know, your parents are meeting with me to work out arrangements following their separation. They would like to you to have a chance to say how you feel about it and to put forward any suggestions or wishes you may have, so that arrangements can be worked out by all of you together.

Mediators help family members to listen to each other, understand each other's point of view and work things out by agreement, without the mediator taking sides or making decisions.

I should be glad to hear how things are going from your point of view and whether there are any changes that you think would work better. I won't ask you to make choices or decisions and I am not a social worker who writes reports and advises the judge. I often talk with young people whose parents live apart and they say they like talking and it helps them to feel better.

Our conversation would be confidential (except where a child is at risk of harm) and I would only share a message or suggestion that you would like me to share with your parents and not tell them any more than this. Your parents won't tell you what you should say to me and they have also promised not to ask you afterwards what you said and be upset with you.

If you would like to have a talk, either online or meeting in person where I work, please could you let me know by text or email and suggest when would be a good day and time for you, or ask one of your parents to let me know.

With best wishes and hoping to hear from you,

....

Family Mediator

Appendix E

Draft letter to son/daughter-in-law regarding grandparents' contact

Dear ……

I am a family mediator and I have been approached by……X…… who, as you may know, is seeking to have some contact with ….Y…. (their grandchild).

X…… has explained that s/he believes you are not in favour of this contact taking place and does not think you will be willing to discuss it. I hope, however, that we can have a word about it. I should be glad to know what you think would be best for ….. and to discuss this with you on your own, privately and in confidence.

I hope you will contact me by email or on my mobile ……… so that we can speak on the phone and perhaps arrange to meet.

I believe …X…… would prefer to avoid court proceedings, if possible. When there are court proceedings, the court expects each party to attend an information meeting with a family mediator before court proceedings take place.

I would not make a charge for a phone conversation. An information meeting is free of charge for those eligible for legal aid and there is a voucher scheme that covers the costs of mediation sessions up to £500, where at least one of the participants qualifies for legal aid.

Hoping to hear from you,

Yours sincerely

Accredited family mediator

Appendix F

Books for children and young people

Some of these books may be out of print and available only second hand – and of course there are new books coming out all the time.

Books for young children

Brown, Laurene Krasny and Marc, *Dinosaurs Divorce – a Guide for Changing Families.* Parents and young children enjoy this book a lot and find it very helpful.

Baum, Louis, *Are we nearly there?* A short story about a little boy who is reluctant to end his time with his father and reassured that they will meet again soon.

Bright, Rachel, *The Worrysaurus.*

Chandler, Richy K, *You make your parents super happy!* A book aimed at 3–5-year-olds that has very good reviews from parents – beautifully simple and quirky illustrations.

Cole, Babette, *Two of Everything.* A bit crazy, with funny drawings.

Cole, Elizabeth, *My Way to Keep Anger Away.* Aimed at quite a wide age range, a book about anger management strategies.

Cole, Julia, *How do I feel about my Parents' Divorce.* For ages 5–11.

De Smet, Marian and Talsma, Nynke *I have Two Homes.* A picture book for 4–6 year-olds – beautiful illustrations and lovely overall message – also addresses some problems that come up in some families – translated from Dutch.

Gray, Kes, *Mum and Dad Glue.* For young children – sad, but with a consoling message, also *Worries Go away* – another rhyming picture book, not specifically about separation/divorce.

Ironside, Virginia, *The Huge Bag of Worries.*

Masurel, Claire, *Two Homes.* A gentle and positive book for 4– 7-year-olds.

Morrissey, Sharon, *That's Not My Ending!*

Peters, Steve, *My Hidden Chimp – helping children to understand their emotions, thinking and behaviour.*

Powell, Jillian, *Family Break-Up What do we think about it.* Helpful text with photographs of children of different ages and ethnicity and a useful glossary.

Schab, Lisa M, *Divorce Workbook for Teens.* A self-help book by a US social worker for teenagers whose parents are divorcing – may be suitable for younger children.

Smith, Samantha and Linda, *Divorce Survival Guide for Kids: Tips to Survive Your Parents' Divorce: For Kids, Written by Kids.* A survival guide written by two sisters whose parents divorced and the girls found they were the 'go-to' source of information for their peers. Practical and positive.

Stones, Rosemary and Spoor, Nicola, *Children don't divorce.*

Striker, Susan and Kimmel, Edward, *The Anti-Colouring Book.* Encourages imagination and expression of feelings.

Thomas, Pat and Harker, Lesley, *My Family's Changing.*

Tobin, Ashley, *Emotion Detective.* A new daily feelings journal for children, including coping strategies.

Vigna, Judith, *Saying Goodbye to Daddy.* Helps young children to move between separated parents.

For older children and teenagers

Grunsell, Angela, *Let's Talk about Stepfamilies.*

Lamb, Kathryn, *Is Anyone's Family as Mad as Mine? – A Survival Guide for Teenagers.* Not about separation/divorce, funny and very good on teenager-parent communication.

Morris, Emily, *It's Not the End.* A booklet for young people about separation/divorce, with helpful information and suggestions. Emily wrote this booklet while at school, drawing from her own experience. Available as a free download: www.fixers.org.uk/index.phpmodule_instance_id=11312&core_alternate_io_handler=view_fixer_printable&data_ref_id=10948&printable_num=1.

Rudkin A and Fitzgerald R, *Split Survival Kit – 10 steps for coping with your parents' separation.*

Stones, Rosemary, *It's Not Your Fault – What to Do When Your Parents Divorce.* Suitable for children around 10–14 who like reading.

Swan-Jackson, Alys *Caught in the Middle – Teenagers Talk about their Parents' Divorce*

DVDs and websites

www.itsnotyourfault.co.uk, 'to help you understand family break-up and feel a bit better'.

Cafcass, 'My Family's Changing' www.cafcass.gov.uk.

McGhee, Christina, *Lemons 2 Lemonade: how to handle life when things go sour between Mom and Dad.* DVD and workbook designed for children 5–12 years old, available online at www.divorceandchildren.com.

NACC's website (National Association of Child Contact Centres) has a section for children and young people.

Shout – UK's 24/7 Crisis Text Service for Mental Health Support | Shout 85258 (giveusashout.org)

www.teenagehealthfreak.org, health information and advice for teenagers, includes a page on divorce.

Fiction for children and young people

Balen K, *October, October* and *The Light in Everything.*

Blume, Judy, *It's not the End of the World.*

Fine, Anne, *Madame Doubtfire*. For older children, enjoyed by parents too, also *Goggle Eyes* – by a teenager about her reactions to her mum's new boyfriend and how this changes and *Step by wicked step* – stepchildren tell their stories to each other.

Palacio, R.J., *Wonder ('You can't blend in when you were born to stand out')*. Coping with disfigurement and bullying – powerful and life-affirming.

Stark-McGinnis, Sandy, *Extraordinary Birds*. Told by a girl in foster care who knows two things: (1) about birds; (2) how to get kicked out of foster homes. Stunning!

Wilson, Jacqueline, *The Suitcase Kid*, also *Clean Break, Sleep-overs, Love Lessons, Secrets* and many more.

Appendix G

Some suggested reading that mediators may find useful – or just enjoy!

Adie K *Nobody's Child – Who are you when you don't know your past*? (Hodder & Stoughton, 2005)

Clegg B *Did You Ever Have A Family?* (Vintage Books, 2016)

Clanchy K *Antigona and Me* (Picador, 2008)'

– *Some Kids I Taught and What They Taught Me* (Picador, 2019)

Fine A *Madame Doubtfire* (Penguin Books, 1989)

– *Goggle-eyes* (Picador, 1987) narrated by a teenager

– *Step by wicked step* (Puffin Books, 1996) stepchildren tell their stories

Gerhardt S *Why Love Matters – how affection shapes a baby's brain* (Routledge, 2004)

Grant C and D *A Very Modern Family: Stories and Guidance to Nurture Your Relationships* (Piatkus Publishing, 2023)

Higashida N *The Reason I Jump* (Hodder & Stoughton, 2013)

James H *What Maisie Knew* (first published 1897)

Kay J *Trumpet* (Picador, 1998)

– *Red Dust Road* (Picador, 2010)

Keegan C *Foster* (Faber paperbacks, 2022)

Palacio R.J. *Wonder – you can't blend in when you were born to stand out* (Corgi, 2013)

Sheldrake M *Entangled Life* (Vintage Books, Penguin, 2020)

Sissay L *My Name is Why* (Canongate, 2019)

Stark-McGinnis S *Extraordinary Birds* (Bloomsbury, 2019)

Winterson J *Oranges Are Not The Only Fruit* (Pandora Press, 1985)

– *Why Be Happy When You Could be Normal?* (Vintage Books, 2012)

Bibliography

Abarbanel, A, 'Shared parenting after separation and divorce: a study of joint custody' (1979) 49 *American Journal of Orthopsychiatry.*

Adam, H, 'Time for Climate Change in the Family Justice System' [2022] *Family Law* 996.

Adie, K *Nobody's Child – Who are you when you don't know your past?* (Hodder & Stoughton, 2005).

Ainsworth, M and Wittig, B, 'Attachment and exploratory behavior of one year olds in a strange situation' in B M Foss (ed), *Determinants of Infant Behavior IV* (Methuen 1969).

– 'Attachment: Retrospect and Prospect' in C M Parkes and J Stevenson-Hinde (eds), *The Place of Attachment in Human Behaviour* (Basic Books, 1982).

Bane, M J, 'Marital disruption and the lives of children' (1976) 32 *Journal of Social Issues.*

Barlow, A, Ewing J et al., *Mapping Paths to Family Justice – Briefing Paper and Report on Key Findings* (Universities of Exeter and Kent, June 2014);

– *An Evaluation of Mediation in Mind* (Final Report, University of Exeter June 2020).

Barn, R et al., *Parenting in Multi-Racial Britain* (National Children's Bureau and Joseph Rowntree Foundation, July 2006).

Baron-Cohen, S, *Zero Degrees of Empathy* (Penguin Books, 2011).

Bateson, G, *Small Arcs of Larger Circles* (Triarchy Press, 2016).

Bendall, C and Davey, S, 'The Grandparent 'Problem' – Encouraging a more relational approach to child arrangements via mediation' in Davey and Lindsey (eds), *Grandparents and the Law – Rights and Relationships* (Hart Publishing, 2023).

Beausoleil, E, 'Dance and Neuroscience – Implications for Conflict Transformation' in LeBaron, McLeod and Acland (eds), *The Choreography of Resolution – Conflict, Movement and Neuroscience* (American Bar Association, 2013)

Blakemore, S-J, *How to help nurture teenage minds, The Guardian,* 11 March 2023.

– *Inventing Ourselves: The Secret Life of the Teenage Brain* (Black Swan, 2018)

Bonadotta, M and Farinacci, P, 'Ascoltare I figli di separati nei Gruppi di Parola' in Bramanti and Marzotto (eds), *Ascoltare lasciando traccia* (Vita e Pensiero, 2019).

Bowlby, J *Attachment and Loss* (Basic Books, 1969).

– *The Making and Breaking of Affectional Bonds* (Routledge, 1989).

Brown, L K and Brown, M, *Dinosaurs Divorce – A Guide for Changing Families* (Dino Life Guides, 1988).

Bryant, D, *An Australian perspective on the Family Justice Review* (International Family Law Lecture, London 2012).

Cafcass, Annual Report 2006–2007.

Cafcass *Parenting Plan* www.cafcass.gov.uk/grown-ups/parenting-plan.aspx https://www.cafcass.gov.uk/2023/02/09/cafcass-publishes-new-tips-from-its-family-forum-for-parents-and-professionals-involved-in-the-family-court/.

Caratsch, C, *Resolving Family Conflicts – a Guide to International Family Mediation* (International Social Service, Geneva, 2014).

Cassidy, D and Davey, S, *Family Justice Children's Proceedings, Research Summary* (Ministry of Justice 2011) 5/11.

Centre of Expertise on Child Sexual Abuse https://www.csacentre.org.uk/knowledge-in-practice/practice-improvement/communicating-with-children-guide/.

Chan, M J, *Bright Fear* (Faber, 2023).

Childline Report, *Unhappy Parents, Unhappy Children,* 1998.

Clanchy, K, *Antigona and Me* (Picador, 2008)

Cloke, K, *Mediation and meditation: the deeper middle way,* mediate.com Weekly 2009, no. 266.

Cockett, M and Tripp, J, *The Exeter Family Study: family breakdown and its impact on children* (Exeter University Press, 1994).

Cohen, L and Campos, J, 'Father, mother and stranger as elicitors of attachment behaviour in infants' (1974) 10 *Journal of Developmental Psychology.*

Committee on One-Parent Families, 'Finer Report', HMSO 1974.

Coram Foundation, *Building Brighter Futures – Empowering children with the skills and aspiration they need to thrive* (Autumn 2023 Newsletter).

Council of Europe, Recommendation *Family mediation and gender equality,* No. 1639, 2003. – *Guidelines on Child-Friendly Justice,* 2010.

Culpin, I et al., 'Father absence and depressive symptoms in adolescence' (2013) 43(12) *Journal of Psychological Medicine.*

Daniel, B, Wassell, S and Gilligan, R, 'It's just common sense, isn't it? Exploring ways of putting the theory of resilience into action' (1999) 23(3) *Adoption and Fostering.*

Darwin, C, *Origin of Species.*

Defoe, D, A *Tour Through the Whole Island of Great Britain 1724-27.*

Department for Education *The Munro Review of Child Protection – a child-centred system 2011; Working Together to Safeguard Children, 2018; Statutory guidance on inter-agency working to safeguard and promote the welfare of children* (2015, updated February 2019).

De Souza, R, *Briefing on Children's Mental Health Services 2020/21.*

Donaldson, M, *Children's Minds* (Fontana Press, 1987).

Donne, J, 'The Relique' in J Robbins (ed), *The Complete Poems of John Donne.*

Dunn, J and Deater-Deckard, K, 'Children's views of their changing families' (Joseph Rowntree Research findings, 2011) 931.

Elstein, S and Felibert, M P, 'La Escucha de los Ni⊠os en Mediación' *May 2023 La Trama journal*, Argentina.

Emery, R, *The Truth about Children and Divorce* (Viking, 2004).

Emery, R et al., Child Custody Mediation and Litigation: Custody, Contact and Co-parenting twelve years after initial dispute resolution (2001) 69(2) *Journal of Consulting and Clinical Psychology* 323–32

Enright, A, *The Wren, the Wren* (Jonathan Cape, 2023).

Erikson, E, *Childhood and Society* (Norton & Co, 1950).

European Commission 13th Forum on the Rights of the Child 2020 (europa.eu).

Ewing, J, 'What About Me? Do we have the 'right' approach to children when parents separate?' [2021] *Family Law.*

Family Justice Council and Family Mediation Council, *Guide to Family Mediation in England and Wales,* April 2014.

Family Mediation Council Code of Practice for Mediators, 2016, 2018.

– Professional Standards and Self-Regulatory Framework, updated 2019

– Survey of Members, January 2020.

– Report to National Audit Office Consultation on Legal Aid, July 2023.

Family Mediation Council *FMC-Manual-of-Professonal-Standards-Regulatory-Framework-v1.3-Updated-June-2019;* www.familymediationcouncil.org.uk/wp-content/uploads/2022/08/FMC-MIAM-Standards-August-2022.

Family Solutions Group Report, *What About Me? Reframing Support for Families following Parental Separation,* 12 November 2020.

Family Solutions Group *What About Me? A Child's Right to Matter* November 2023.

Fiadjoe, A, *Family mediation in the Caribbean* Paper given at the Council of Europe's 7th European Conference on Family Law on International Family Mediation, Strasbourg, March 2009.

Ferri, E and Smith, D, *Step-parenting in the 1990s* (Family Policy Studies Centre, 1996).

Fisher, R and Ury, W, *Getting to Yes- Negotiating Agreement Without Giving In* (Houghton-Mifflin, 1981).

Fine, A, *Step by wicked step* (Puffin Books, 1996).

Finer Committee *Report of the Committee on One-Parent Families* (1974) HMSO Cm 5629.

Fortin, J, Scanlan, L and Hunt, J, 'Taking a longer view of contact: the perspectives of young adults who experienced parental separation in their youth' [2013] *Family Law* 104.

Fraser, A, *The Case of the Married Woman: Caroline Norton and her Fight for Women's Justice* (Pegasus Books, 2022).

Garwood, F, *Children in Conciliation* (Scottish Association of Family Conciliation Services, 1989).

Gerhardt, S, *Why Love Matters – how affection shapes a baby's brain* (Routledge, 2004).

Ghezzi G *La mediazione familiare nel contesto della famiglia adottiva* doctoral thesis 2006, Università Cattolica, Milan.

Gibran, K, *The Prophet* (Heinemann, 1926).

Goldstein, F and Solnit, *Beyond the Best Interests of the Child* (The Free Press, 1973).

Gorin, S, *Understanding what children say: Children's experiences of domestic abuse, parental substance misuse and parental health problems* (Joseph Rowntree Foundation, 2004) 514.

Gov.uk, *Assessing Risk of Harm to Children and Parents in Private Law Children Cases,* 'Harm Report', June 2020.

Grant, C and Grant, D, *A Very Modern Family: Stories and Guidance to Nurture Your Relationships* (Piatkus Publishing, 2023).

Gray, A, 'The changing availability of grandparents as carers and its implications for childcare in the UK' (2005) 34(4) *Journal of Social Policy.*

Hague Conference, *Guide to Good Practice on Mediation in the context of the 1980 Child Abduction Convention,* July 2012.

Hale, B, *Spider Woman – A Life* (Penguin Books, 2021).

Harold, G et al., *What Works to Enhance Inter-Parental Relationships and Improve Outcomes for Children* (Early Intervention Foundation, 2016).

Harold, G and Sellers, R, 'Inter-parental Conflict and Youth Psychopathology; an Evidence Review and Practice Focused Update' (2018) 59(4) *Journal of Child Psychology and Psychiatry.*

Hawthorne, J, Pryor and Richards, *Supporting children through family change* (Joseph Rowntree Foundation Findings, 2003) 323.

Hayes, S, 'Family Mediators in the UK – A Survey of Practice' [2002] *Family Law* 760.

Haynes, J, *Divorce Mediation* (Springer Publishing, 1981).

Higashida, N, *The Reason I Jump* (English edn, Hodder & Stoughton, 2013).

Hodgson, L-G, 'Adult grandchildren and their grandparents: the enduring bond' (1992) 34(3) *International Journal of Ageing and Human Development* 209–25.

Hunt, J, *Parental Perspectives on the Family Justice System in England and Wales: a review of research* (Report for the Family Justice Council, December 2009).

James, H, *What Maisie Knew* (Penguin Classics, 1986).

Johnston, J and Roseby, V, *In the Name of the Child: a developmental approach to understanding and helping children of conflicted and violent divorce* (Free Press, 1997).

Kanneh-Mason, K, *The House of Music* (Oneworld, 2020).

Kauser, S, 'Mediation and Cultural Diversity' [2022] *Family Law.*

Kay, J, *Trumpet* (Picador, 1998).

Kedward C, Luckock B and Lawson H *Mediation and post-adoption contact* Adoption and Fostering 1999 vol. 23, no 3.

Keshavjee, M, *Islam, Sharia and Alternative Dispute Resolution* (IB Tauris, 2013).

Lamb, K, *Is Anyone's Family as Mad as Mine? A Survival Guide for Teenagers* (Piccadilly Press, 2006).

Lamb, M, *Father-infant and mother-infant interaction in the first year of life Child Development* 1977, 48.

Langford, W et al., *Family understandings: Closeness, authority and independence in families with teenagers* (Family Policy Studies Centre, March 2001).

Lansdown, G, *Promoting children's participation in democratic decision-making* (UNICEF/Innocenti, Florence, Italy, 2001).

Lansdown G *The evolving capacities of the child* (Innocenti Research Centre, UNICEF/ Save the Children, Florence 2005).

Law Commission, Review of Child Law: Custody, Working Paper 96, HMSO 1986.

Leach, P, *Family Breakdown* (Unbound, 2014).

Lewis, P and Warin, *Cohabitation, separation and fatherhood* (Joseph Rowntree Foundation Findings, 2002) 552.

Lively, P, *The Driftway* (Heinemann, 1972).

Lowe N et al *Supporting Adoption, Reframing the Approach* 1999, British Association of Adoption and Fostering (BAAF).

Lyon, C, Surrey, E and Timms, J, *Effective Support Services for Children' and young people when parental relationships break down – a child-centred approach* (University of Liverpool, 1998).

Locke, J, *Some Thoughts Concerning Education,* 1693.

Marzotto, C (ed) *Gruppi di parola per figli di genitori separati* (Vita e Pensiero, 2010).

McCarthy, P and Walker, J, *The longer-term impact of family mediation* (Joseph Rowntree Findings, 1996) 103.

McFarlane, A, *Supporting Families in Conflict – there is a better way,* Address to the Jersey Family Law Conference, 2021.

McIntosh, J, Smyth, F, Kelaher, Wells and Long, *Post-separation parenting arrangements and developmental outcomes for infants and children* (Family Court of Australia, Attorney-General's Department, 2010).

'Child-Focused and Child-Inclusive Divorce Mediation: Comparative Outcomes' (2008) 46(1) *Family Courts Review,* Association of Family and Conciliation Courts.

McIntosh, J, Wells, Y and Long, C, 'Child-focused and child-inclusive family law dispute resolution' (2007) 13(1) *Journal of Family Studies.*

Ministry of Justice *Mediation Task Force Report June 2014 Supporting earlier resolution of private family law arrangements* April 2023 www.gov.uk.

Mirk, J, 'Mirk's Festial – a Collection of Homilies' published in *English Sermons 1100 – 1500* (Early English Text Society, Kegan Paul, 1905).

Miyake, K et al., 'Infant Temperament, Mothers' Mode of Interaction, and Attachment in Japan' (1985) 50 *Monographs of the Society for Research in Child Development* 276–97.

Ministry of Justice Green, Paper *Legal Aid Reform 2010.*

– Family Justice Review Final Report, 'Norgrove Report', 2011.

– Mediation Task Force Report, 2014.

Mitchell, A, *Children in the Middle* (Tavistock, 1985).

Morrow, V, 'Children's Perspectives on Families' (Joseph Rowntree Research Findings, 1998) 798.

Murch, M, *Justice and Welfare in Divorce* (Sweet and Maxwell, 1980).

Murch, M and Keehan, G, 'The Voice of the Child in Private Family Law Proceedings' [2003] *Family Law.*

Murray Parkes, C and Stevenson-Hinde, J, *The Place of Attachment in Human Behaviour* (Tavistock Publications, 1982).

Nash, J M, Fertile minds (1997) 149(5) *Time 1.*

Neale, B and Wade, A, *Parent Problems! Children's views on life when parents split up* (Young Voice, 2000).

Nord, C, *The Balanced Brain: The Science of Mental Health* (Allen Lane, 2023).

Norton, C, *English Laws for Women in the 19th century* (Dodo Press {DATE}.

Office of the Children's Commissioner, *Do More than Listen, Act.* Consultation Response, July 2011.

Office for National Statistics, *Children's views on well-being and what makes a happy life* ons.gov.uk, 2020.

O'Quigley, A, *Listening to Children's Views* (Joseph Rowntree Foundation, 2000).

Parkinson, L, *Joint Custody* One Parent Times October 1981.

– *Conciliation in Separation and Divorce* (Croom Helm, 1986, reissued Routledge, 2023).

– *Family Mediation* (1st edn, Grant McIntyre, 1997, 4th edn, LexisNexis, 2020).

– 'Child-Inclusive Family Mediation' [2006] *Family Law.*

– 'Adults should talk to kids more' [2012] *Family Law.*

– 'Are You Listening? Conversations with children during parental separation and divorce' [2021] *Family Law.*

– 'Ecosystemic family mediation' [2022] *Family Law.*

– Mediation with grandparents August [2023] *Family Law.*

Partnership for Multi-Ethnic Inclusion, *Social Linkworking and Inter-Cultural Mediation in Europe* (eds. Molina et al), PfMI, Sweden 2001.

Paul, C and Kiesewetter, S, *Cross-border Family Mediation* (Wolfgang Metzner Verlag, Frankfurt-am-Main 2011). Paul C, Kiesewetter, S and Khalaf-Newsome, I (eds), (3rd edn, 2023).

Place, M, 'Attachment and Identity – their significance in decisions about contact and placement' [2003] *Family Law.*

Rapoport, R, 'The state of crisis – some theoretical considerations' in Parad (ed), *Crisis Intervention* (Family Service Association of America, 1965).

Reynolds, J et al., *Parental Conflict: Outcomes and interventions for children and families* (Policy Press and Research Paper, University of Southampton, 2014).

Richardson, M, 'Parental alienation in the vital early stages of litigation' [2019] *Family Law.*

Richman, J and Bowen, L, 'School failure: an interactional ecological developmental perspective' in Fraser, M (ed), *Risk and Resilience in Childhood: an ecological perspective* (NASW Press, 1997).

Rilling, J et al, *The neural correlates of grandmaternal caregiving* (Proceedings of the Royal Society B: Biological Sciences, November 2021).

Roberts, M, *Mediation in Family Disputes* (Community Care Practice Handbooks 1988).

Robinson, L, *Cross-cultural child development for social workers – an introduction* (Palgrave, 2007).

Royal Australian College of Physicians, *Health of children in 'out-of-home' care* (RACP, 2006).

Rundell, K *Super-Infinite – the Transformations of John Donne* (Faber & Faber, 2022).

Rutter, M, 'Resilience in the Face of Adversity' (1985) 147 *British Journal of Psychiatry.*

Schaefer et al., 'The health-related functions of social support' (1981) 4 *Journal of Behavioral Medicine* 381–406.

Schaffer, H, Rudolph *Making Decisions about Children – Psychological Questions and Answers* (Blackwell, 1990).

Schore, A and McIntosh, J, 'Family Law and the neuroscience of attachment', Part 1 [2011] *Family Court Review* 49.

Scrive, A, 'Médiation familiale et reprise des liens' in Eid and Scrive (eds), Être grand-parent – Entre présence et distance (Chronique social, 2015).

Smart, C, 'From Children's Shoes to Children's Voices' (2002) 30(3) *Family Court Review.*

– 'Equal shares: rights for fathers or recognition for children?' [2004] *Critical Social Policy* 484.

– 'It's My Life Too- Children's Perspectives on Post-Divorce Parenting' [2000] *Family Law.*

Smart, C and Neale, B, *Family Fragments?* (Polity Press, 1999).

Steinman, S, 'The Experience of Children in a Joint Custody Arrangement' (1981) 51 *American Journal of Orthopsychiatry* 403–14.

The Lancet Child and Adolescent Health, *Adolescent Well-being in the UK,* September 2021.

Th⊠rnblad and Strandbu, 'The Involvement of Children in the Process of Mandatory Family Mediation' in Nylund et al. (eds), *Nordic Mediation Research* (Springer Books, 2018).

Timms, N, *The Silent Majority – the Position of Children Involved in the Divorce and Separation of their Parents* (Child Care in Practice, April 2003).

Townsend, S, *The Secret Diary of Adrian Mole aged 13¾* (Methuen, 1982).

Trinder, L, *Making Contact happen or making contact work? The process and outcomes of in-court conciliation* (DCA Research Series 2006) 3/06.

– 'Conciliation, the Private Law Programme and Children's Well-being' [2008] *Family Law* 338.

– 'Shared Residence: a review of recent research evidence' [2010] *Family Law.*

Trinder, L, Beek, M and Connolly, J, *Children's and parents' experience of contact after divorce* (Joseph Rowntree Foundation Research Findings, 2002) 092.

Tronick, E Z et al., 'The Efe Forager Infant and Toddler Patterns of Social Relationships – Multiple and Simultaneous' (1992) 28 *Journal of Developmental Psychology* 568–77.

UK College of Family Mediators, *Children, Young People and Family Mediation – Policy and Practice Guidelines,* 2000.

UN Committee on the Rights of the Child, *Report and Concluding Observations* 2 June 2023.

University of Exeter Wellcome Centre, Healthy Relationships Project, *Report and Key Findings,* March 2022.

University of Exeter, *The Rights Idea? Network on Family Regulation and Society.*

United Nations Convention on the Rights of the Child 1989.

Van Hamelin, A L, *Resilience – a complexity science approach* (In Conversation, ACAMH, 2023).

Voice of the Child Advisory Group Report, March 2015.

Walker, J, McCarthy, P and Timms, N, *Mediation: the Making and Remaking of Co-operative Relationships,* (Relate Centre for Family Studies, University of Newcastle, 1994).

Walker, J and H, J, *Communication in Marriage and Divorce* (The BT Forum, 1996).

Wallerstein, J and Kelly, J, *Surviving the Break-Up – how children and parents cope with divorce* (Grant McIntyre, 1980).

Wallerstein, J, 'Long-term effects of divorce on children' (1991) 30 *Journal of American Academy of Child and Adolescent Psychiatry* 3.

Whitcombe, S, 'Parental Alienation or Justifiable Estrangement? Assessing a Child's Resistance to a Parent in the UK' (2017) 27(3) *Seen and Heard.*

Wiley, 'Parental alienation: where are we now?' [2019] *Family Law.*

Wilson, J, *The Suitcase Kid* (Corgi Books, 1992).

Woodall, K and Woodall, N, *Understanding Parental Alienation* (Charles C. Thomas, 2017).

Yates, P and Allardyce, S, *Sibling sexual abuse – A Knowledge and Practice Overview* (Centre of Expertise on Child Sexual Abuse, January 2021).

Young, E, *They, Them, Their – a guide to nonbinary and genderqueer identities* (Jessica Kingsley 2019)

Young Minds, NHS Digital, April 2022.

Yousafzai, M, *I Am Malala* (Phoenix Books, 2013).

Index

References are to page number.